A Pictorial History of
HORROR MOVIES

And the Prophet said –
And lo, the Beast looked
Upon the face of Beauty.
And it stayed its hand
From killing. And from that
Day, it was as one dead.

Old Arabian Proverb
KING KONG (1933)

Half-title page: *House of Dark Shadows* (MGM 1970)
Title page: *The Ghost of Frankenstein* (Universal 1942)
Quotations page: *Terror in the Midnight Sun* (Unger 1963)
Introduction page: *The Bat* (Liberty 1959)
            Black Sabbath (Galatea 1963)

For Pandora Jane – one day.
Meanwhile in memory of
Bryan Berry
for whom *The Witching Hour*
sounded too soon.

A Pictorial History of

HORROR MOVIES

Denis Gifford

NEW YORK

First published in USA 1984
by Exeter Books

Distributed by Bookthrift
Exeter is a trademark of Simon & Schuster, Inc.
Bookthrift is a registered trademark of Simon & Schuster, Inc.
New York, New York

ISBN 0-671-06936-5

Printed in Hong Kong

Also by Denis Gifford:
British Cinema
Movie Monsters
Science Fiction Film
Discovering Comics
Stap Me! The British Newspaper Strip
Six Comics of World War One
Test Your N.Q. (Nostalgia Quotient)
Fifty Years of Radio Comedy
The British Film Catalogue

CONTENTS

I tell you, we haven't begun to discover
what science can do to the body and mind of man
HENRY JEKYLL MD (John Barrymore) 1920

Think of it! The brain of a dead man, waiting to live again
in a body I made with my own hands!
HENRY FRANKENSTEIN (Colin Clive) 1931

Feast your eyes, gloat your soul, on my
accursed ugliness!
THE PHANTOM (Lon Chaney) 1925

This is the greatest moment of my life!
I have seen a living pterodactyl!
PROFESSOR CHALLENGER (Wallace Beery) 1925

I took a gorilla and, working with infinite care,
I made my first man!
DR MOREAU (Charles Laughton) 1932

Mad? I, who have solved the secret of life,
you call me mad?
DR OTTO VON NIEMANN (Lionel Atwill) 1933

It was Beauty killed the Beast!
CARL DENHAM (Robert Armstrong) 1933

I meddled in things that man must leave alone!
JACK GRIFFIN (Claude Rains) 1933

Alone you have created a man. Now together
we will create his mate!
DR PRETORIUS (Ernest Thesiger) 1935

The werewolf instinctively seeks to kill
the thing it loves best!
DR YOGAMI (Warner Oland) 1935

We belong dead!
THE FRANKENSTEIN MONSTER (Boris Karloff) 1935

To die! To be really dead!
That must be glorious!
COUNT DRACULA (Bela Lugosi) 1931

INTRODUCTION

WHEN IS A HORROR FILM NOT A HORROR FILM?

They were giants in the night: two tall men in two tall hats who swung out and away from each other and came at me, striding from the colossal window. And if I hadn't screamed and ducked under the seat they would have trampled me into the ice-cream wrappers. The site was the outsize Trocadero Cinema at the Elephant and Castle, London; the sight was no more than two top-hatted toffs, probably Jack Hulbert and Jack Buchanan, bidding themselves bye-bye; the night was the winter of 1930; the mite was yours truly the horror film fan; and the fright was simply dimensional – magnification plus depth. I in my three-year-old innocence was reacting classically to the concept of cinema, just as those first, older innocents had shrieked and shied from old Lumière's film of an oncoming engine, back in the beyond of 1895.

My early movie memories are all of horror: a long rifle nosing through the flap of a big top tent to pick off a man on a flying trapeze; two cowboys slugging away in the back of a jolting lorry as it racketed around a rocky mountain; a zoom into the open mouth of a cartoon character to see a similar face grimacing on its uvula. Horrid moments, yet not horror films.

I brushed the real thing but once in my bare-kneed days before the British Censor saved me with his 'H' for Horrific Certificate. Mum, daringly, considering all the embarrassing seat-banging she had been through, took me to see *The Invisible Man*. The experience was a treasured shudder for years, and now that I have my own print of it, I love the film all the more. For the curious thing about all the great horror films . . . *Frankenstein, Dracula, King Kong, The Old Dark House* . . . is that they are not only good for a first-time thrill, they can be seen again and again, savoured, rolled around the eyeballs. Unlike most movies they actually improve with the years, outmoded acting and production techniques adding a mouldering charm to the vintage. Where once *Dracula* was criticized for its contemporary setting, now it has developed a period crust of its own. Perhaps time will add its own patina to the Hammer horrors of today.

The Golden Age of the Horror Film passed me by as a direct experience, for once I was old enough to be allowed in by commissionaires with eagle-eyes for under-sixteens, the great days were over. I had to rely on that other curious British institution, the Sunday-For-One-Day-Only reissue bill. I sought out every side-street flea-pit for those treasured double-bills: *Buried Alive* and *The Monster Maker*, or *Devil Bat's Daughter* and *Mask of the Maniac*. I began to take notes, collect stills, collate press-books. Friends of a like mind joined me in winkling out films and facts. Bob Monkhouse, who became a star comedian, stirred my schoolboy zeal with tales of films seen surreptitiously in Worthing; Tony Hawes, who became a star writer, led me to tatty bug-hutches in wild Lee Green; Jennifer Jayne, who in time actually acted in horror films, came along for the fun; Bryan Berry, who became a great science-fiction novelist, helped me adapt remembered movies into playlets; Len Lurcuck, who became a TV director, supplied our sound effects; David Kodritsch, who draws maps for the War House, put on my imported Frankenstein Monster mask and stomped round the garden to be photographed. I wrote the history of Horror Films twenty years ago, but nobody wanted to know (until Carlos Clarens finally came through with the right book at the right time). I created the first Horror Film magazine and called it 'H' – but nobody wanted to know (until Forrest J. Ackerman finally came through with the right mag at the right time). I even drew a horror comic, but nobody etc. etc. (until William Gaines finally etc. etc.). So you see, horror films and I are no strange bedfellows.

Yet ask me to define a horror film and I am stumped. Even the British Board of Film Censors, who actually officially christened the things with the creation of their 'H' Certificate, never got around to defining them. Witness the anomalies in their list which I append to this volume: *Boy Slaves? The United Nations War Crimes Film*? Egads! You'll find no mention of them in the text. Nor will you find movies with mere moments of horror, like *Psycho* or the descendants of *Les Diaboliques*. For me, an element of fantasy is essential to the true horror film: the impossible rather than the improbable. The vampire, the werewolf, the walking dead and the man-made monster – these are the heroes of horror films, not the Lodgers and the Rippers and the Hooded Terrors. But fear not, friends, for to trace the history of horror I have cast my web wide, digging deep in the cinematic sarcophagi to disinter long-dead ghosts of films and film-makers forgotten. Perhaps some are still forgotten, by myself: then I'm sorry.

And so I present to you this picture book, with the words of Professor Bruno Lampini, as portrayed by George Zucco in *House of Frankenstein*: 'I have here a collection of the world's most astounding horrors!'

HOW GRAND WAS MY GUIGNOL

In which Monsieur Méliès summons the Devil, Mr Smith photographs a ghost, Mr Porter takes a shot in the dark, and Quasimodo gets the hump.

The big, black bat flew into the castle room. It circled slowly, flapping monstrous wings. Suddenly – it changed into the Devil! It was the eve of Christmas 1896; the horror had begun.

Regular patrons of the little Théâtre Robert Houdin on the second floor of No. 8 Boulevard des Italiens, in Paris, were used to magic. For eight years now the prestidigitating proprietor had staged the most astonishing sequence of theatrical illusions ever seen: disappearances, decapitations, devilry undreamed by even the great Etienne Robertson, whose *Phantasmagoria* had brought horror to the magic lantern a hundred years before.

But now even Monsieur Méliès had excelled himself. Seizing upon the new scientific apparatus invented by the brothers Lumière – a machine to record movement by rapid photography they called *le cinématographe* – Méliès incorporated it into his act. Where once mere handfuls of Parisians had thrilled to the magician's trickery, now the world was his audience. Ordinary folk who had paid their pennies to gaze at 'Animated Photographs' of such mundane things as high tide at Brighton and rush hour at Piccadilly, gasped in fright as the bat flew and Satan laughed. In *The Devil's Castle* (1896) Mephistopheles made a magic pass.

'A large cauldron appears, out of which, in a great cloud of smoke, there emerges a beautiful lady. At another magic pass, a little old man comes out of the floor carrying a big book. Then the cauldron disappears. And so it goes. Cavaliers, ghosts, a skeleton and witches appear and disappear at a sign from the Evil One. Finally, one of the cavaliers produces a cross, and Mephistopheles throws up his hands and disappears in a cloud of smoke. From start to finish the action is rapid.'

It would have to be: the whole film ran for less than three minutes!

While the world wondered at the supernatural transformations unreeling so speedily before its boggling eyes, knowing Parisians nodded. They had spotted the twinkle in Satan's eye. For their mustachioed host at a hundred different magical spectaculars since 1888, and the moving picture Mephisto, were one and the same man.

Georges Méliès, former shoe manufacturer and cartoonist, had turned his hobby of spare-time conjuring into a career. It was to reproduce on film one of his favourite stage illusions, *The Vanishing Lady* (1896), that Méliès created the world's first cinematic device. As the magician, Méliès seated his charming victim in a chair and concealed her with his cloak. At this point he 'froze' his position. The cameraman stopped cranking, the lady left the set, and a stagehand slipped a skeleton into her seat. The cameraman continued the crank, Méliès whipped away the cape. When the printed film was projected without the stops and starts: hey presto! the lady vanished!

Audiences everywhere were astounded. They had seen a genuine physical disappearance, a macabre transformation from life to death, before their very eyes. In that split of a second they had seen even more: cinema taking its first step towards art.

Women had screamed the night cinema was born: a locomotive engine seemed to steam from the screen. Louis Lumière's innocent record of an everyday happening, *The Arrival of a Train at La Ciotat Station* (1895), had shock in its realistic approach. The shriek of surprise became a laugh of relief that was echoed around the world: six years later the memory was strong enough to be recalled by Robert Paul in *The Countryman and the Cinematograph* (1901). The scream of fear and the scream of laughter: an emotional combination that rings down the seventy-seven year history of the horror film.

Beautiful Beast: Jean Marais and Josette Day as Jean Cocteau's *Beauty and the Beast* (1945).

Cinema was but one year old when the Devil took over. A public already sated on Lumière's traffic scenes and burning weeds welcomed him with delighted fright. Merry Méliès gave them more of the same. *The Haunted Castle* and *The Laboratory of Mephistopheles* followed in early 1897, using the same sets, costumes and characters as *The Devil's Castle*. Méliès was a clever old devil.

In his country garden at Montreuil, Méliès built himself a movie studio. He designed it as a combination of standard photographer's studio and his own magic theatre. He filled his stage with concealed traps and hidden holes, movable panels and capstans, winches and pulleys: all the practicable impedimenta of the illusionist. He mounted his camera on a runway and in no time had created every trick in the movie book: stop-frame action, substitution, superimposition, animation, undercranking, split-screen, dissolves, fades both in and out, model work, miniature work, and the subtitle. Everything the horror film would ever need – including fantastic costume and grotesque makeup.

And in his first year of 1897 the world was startled to see Satan's head detach itself and float around a room (*The Laboratory of Mephistopheles*), a traveller flee in fright when his clothes came to life (*The Bewitched Inn*), a mesmerist put a girl in a trance and magically strip her naked (*The Hypnotist at Work*), a scientist use an X-Ray machine to extract the skeleton from a living body (*A Novice at X-Rays*), a boy chopped in half (*The Famous Box Trick*), a marble statue come to life (*Pygmalion and Galatea*), the moon zoom down from the sky to swallow a telescope (*The Astronomer's Dream*), and an old man sell his soul to Satan – twice (*Faust and Marguerite* and *The Damnation of Faust*)!

Meanwhile, across the English Channel, Mr Smith was photographing a ghost. This first cinematographical spectre stalked sunny Sussex in September 1898. It was summoned up by the ex-secretary of the Society for Psychical Research, George Albert Smith. Like Méliès, Smith had been both a conjurer and creator of conjurer's illusions. He had also been a hypnotist on the halls, and it was this mesmeric talent that had won him a place with the famous Society. He assisted in a series of spectacular spiritualistic seances that gained national notoriety. The year 1892 saw Smith's sudden disappearance from the Society staff; 1898 the appearance of a startling advertisement. 'The most marvellous films yet done! Protected under patent law!' They were made by George Albert Smith, initially known as G.A.S. Films.

'*Faust and Mephistopheles.* Faust discovered in his study. Mephistopheles appears in a cloud of smoke (fine effect), offers Faust renewal of youth if he will sign bond. As inducement, shows him charming 'vision' of Marguerite at spinning wheel in the garden. Faust hesitates no longer; signs bond; Mephistopheles triumphantly waves a drinking cup, causing it to emit a cloud of smoke, which falls around Faust as he changes to a handsome young man.'

The 'special photographic contrivance', by which Smith also produced a ghost in *The Corsican Brothers* (1898), was double-exposure, a simple method of 'spirit photography' born by accident in the early days of the camera. But that it was new to cinematography is proved by the granting to Smith of a British Patent. This 'Protection in Great Britain and Abroad' was much vaunted, but within weeks Méliès was advertising *The Cave of the Demons* (1898):

'Showing the interior of a cave, in which appear ghosts and skeletons busied in most mysterious proceedings. A young lady suddenly appears, who is immediately surrounded by the apparitions. The rocks and supports of the cavern are clearly seen through the transparencies of the ghosts' forms. A creepy and startling subject.'

Méliès subtitled his first essay into the spirit world '*scène fantastique avec spectres vivants et impalpables*'. Apparently Smith found Méliès equally untouchable, for no legal action was ever attempted. Indeed, the two film-makers shared the same distributor, Charles Urban. This American in London was the first to realize the box-office potential of the catchy title. In *Cléopâtre* (1899) Méliès made 'an old man of diabolical intent' hack a mummy to bits, then resurrected the living lady from a smoking brazier. Urban called it *Robbing Cleopatra's Tomb*. More catchpenny were the titles he gave to *Le Diable au Couvent* (1899) and *La Danse de Feu* (1899): cashing in on contemporary successes they came out as *The Sign of the Cross* and *Haggard's 'She'*.

Méliès, of course, played the Devil in the convent, leaping out of the holy font. He and 'a deformed imp of satanic type' turn themselves into a priest and a choirboy, changing back during the sermon: 'the nuns dispersing quickly in great

Monster Poster: Original advertisement for *Frankenstein* (Universal 1931).

fright'. In the end the ghost of St George appears, and 'overturns His Satanic Majesty, who descends below amid a cloud of smoke'. More serious in style than his earlier Mephistopheliana, Méliès issued an accompanying caution. 'There is not the least action in the film which would be obnoxious or shock the most sensitive audiences'. The first, but certainly not the last, movie producer to try to have it both ways.

Méliès' films link through to the modern horror movie in ways other than technique. *She*, Rider Haggard's 1887 novel, was no horror story, yet it has one classic horror scene: the lovely young Ayesha bathes in the flames of eternal life only to be overdone into incredible old age. It is a transformation scene of a type basic to the horror film, and in seventy-five feet of celluloid, 'coloured in a most surprising and artistic manner increasing the wonderful effects ten-fold', Méliès showed the core of a story which later film-makers would go to greater lengths to tell. A girl arises from a giant saucepan and executes a hasty skirt-dance before a pillar of fire shrivels her into 'a decrepit old hag'.

The outsize insect finds its harbinger in *A Midnight Episode* (1899). A sleeper, lit by the full moon, 'is suddenly awakened by a bug of gigantic proportions crawling over him. This he attacks and destroys, but before again retiring he notices three more climbing up the wall'. The hero shows all the resource of the modern monster exterminator. 'He lights the candle and applies the flame to each, causing them to explode with fine smoke effects.' A spectacular finale of which Inoshira Honda would be proud.

Méliès' influence was world-wide. In America Thomas Edison, having virtually invented the movies, left their production to his staff, Edwin S. Porter. A man with a mechanical turn of mind – he had been both plumber and projectionist – Porter was intrigued by Méliès' methods. Prints were imported and examined, frame by frame. In February 1900 Porter showed his first fantasy fashioned in the Méliès manner. His choice of subject was no more original than his achievement: *Faust and Marguerite* employed stop-motion photography to materialize Mephistopheles, who then used the same trick to summon up a skeleton. From this derivative beginning Porter would, in three years, reshape cinema.

Meanwhile, in London, another man of mystery was at work. Like Méliès, Walter R. Booth was a conjurer; unlike Méliès, national neglect has let the man himself sink into oblivion. Booth's earliest

Organ Gorgon: Vincent Price as *The Abominable Dr Phibes* (1971; *left*), a British-made American International Picture. The organ was designed by Brian Eatwell, the organs by Trevor Crole-Rees.

Bare Bones: George Méliès personally demonstrates that the hand – and the film – is quicker than the eye. Frames from *The Vanishing Lady* (1896; *below*) reduce a mademoiselle to her skeleton in three easy stages.

Skeleton Key: Dry bones have been walking around horror movies for more than seventy years. A lively skeleton was a bedtime surprise in Robert Paul's *Undressing Extraordinary* (1901; *far left*), a graveyard ghost in Pathé's *The Fairy of the Black Rocks* (1905; *below left*) and a shipboard shriek in Shochiku's *Living Skeleton* (1968; *left*). Edgar Allan Poe's 'Mask of the Red Death' hid Lon Chaney's living skull in *The Phantom of the Opera* (Universal 1925; *right*), while Nathaniel Hawthorne's 'Experiment of Dr Heidegger' bleached Mari Blanchard to her bones in *Twice Told Tales* (Admiral 1963; *below*).

film was probably *The Miser's Doom* (1899), made for Robert Paul. It used its spectre seriously: the spirit of a female victim returns to haunt a miser, who instantly dies of shock. Paul's studio at New Southgate was modelled on Méliès, down to the wheeled camera on rails. When trundled forwards during filming, it gave a gradual enlargement to the image, which was then double-exposed. It produced giants in *The Magic Sword* (1901) and *The Voyage of the 'Arctic'* (1903). This latter fantasy featured Cutcliffe-Hyne's popular magazine hero Captain Kettle, and his discovery of the North Pole. Méliès used his trucking device to create the inflating Satan of *The Gigantic Devil*, the *Amazing Colossal Man* of 1902.

Conversely, both men used the same contrivance to produce life in miniature. Booth's *The Cheese Mites* (1901), subtitled 'Lilliputians in a London Restaurant', showed six-inch sailors dancing the hornpipe on a diner's cheese! Méliès' *The Dancing Midget* came a year later and had more charm. Curious to consider that James Whale's miniaturized manikins in *The Bride of Frankenstein* (1935) included a ballerina.

Like Méliès, Booth treated fantasy lightly, but now and then horror broke through. *The Haunted Curiosity Shop* (1901) showed an antiquarian confronted by a living mummy. 'Before he can recover from the surprise this occasions, the wrappings fall away and the living Egyptian stands before him. Slowly the solid flesh melts away till only the bare skeleton remains.' Audiences of 1933 watching *The Mummy* were spared that additional touch of grue when the sight of a crumbling Karloff

Small World: Horror film makers have it both ways. You can shrink your star and enlarge the world, or enlarge your star and shrink the world. Either way the effect is much the same and the only thing guaranteed to expand is the box office. Henry B. Walthall and Rafaela Ottiana reduced Grace Ford to a *Devil Doll* (MGM 1936; *opposite*), Tod Browning's essay in electrical ecology. Atomic explosions expanded Dean Parkin in *War of the Colossal Beast* (American International 1958; *below*), Bert I. Gordon's essay in back-projection, and the Devil materialized in the form of a giant apeman in *Equinox* (Tonylyn 1969; *left*). Georges Méliès, of course, had done it all decades before in *The Gigantic Devil* (1902; *below left*).

taking 'a little walk' sent David Manners insane.

Méliès, too, looked to Egypt for inspiration, and brought a stone sphinx to life to wreak vengeance on the defiler of a temple tomb in *The Oracle of Delphi* (1903). Worse horror was to come. In *The Monster* (1903) an Egyptian Prince bribes a dervish to restore unto him his dead wife. 'Her skeleton begins to move about, and rises. The dervish covers it with a white cloth; a masque conceals its ghostly face.' It begins to dance, then starts to grow: 'its neck assuming enormous proportions, much to the horror of the Prince, who fails to see in this grotesque character the wife whom he seeks.' The twist in the tail is classic. The monster changes into the Princess and the Prince takes her into his arms. 'Removing the veil he finds he has embraced the skeleton.'

Cinema was giving a new, visual form to the traditional horror story at a time when, in print, imaginative literature was meeting an exciting new challenger. Science-fiction, as a label, was unknown. The trend-setting tales of Jules Verne were called 'Imaginary Voyages', while H.G.Wells' novels were publicised as 'Fantastic Romances'. Both authors met, uninvited, in Méliès' *A Trip to the Moon* (1902). Cinema's first sci-fi epic took the cannon-fired space-shell from Verne's 'From the Earth to the Moon' (1865) and the crustaceous Selenites from Wells' 'The First Men in the Moon' (1901). The explosive quality of the latter when struck by explorers' umbrellas was pure Méliès.

In 1903 Edwin S. Porter took a shot in the dark. Into *The Great Train Robbery* he cut a great closeup.

> '*Scene 14:* A life-size picture of Barnes, the leader of the outlaw band, taking aim and firing point-blank at the audience. The resulting excitement is great.'

Indeed it was. For millions of moviegoers it was the first time they had been shot in the eyeballs. The secret of Scene 14 was its full-frontal relationship to the individual onlooker, a dimension of shock that flashed back to that first onrushing train. It went over the head of Méliès then, and now it did so again. For ten more years he marshalled his movies from stage left to stage right, dissolving from tableau to tableau. The head-on approach was not for him. *The Conquest of the Pole* might as well have been made in 1902, not 1912: Méliès as Engineer Mabouloff flying his Aerobus to battle the Giant of the Snows, an ogre articulated

to the eyeballs and operated by a score of stage-hands. This prehistoric King Kong was a swan song. The old alchemist's audience had grown beyond him; magic was no longer enough.

Georges Méliès, cinema's first producer, director, screen-writer and star, became cinema's first forgotten man. George Barnes had fired a pistol in the world's face and punctured the cardboard dream.

Cinema, born in a French salon, weaned in a London Polytechnic, misspent its youth in a fairground. It grew lustily, pulling in crowds bigger than its neighbour, that other sideshow where people paid to gape – the freak tent. Here nature's pathetic discards eked a living by sitting and being stared at. Naturally, the newest art, being of and by and for the people, absorbed a little of the freak show's aura.

The favourite French fable of Beauty and the Beast had reached its literary apotheosis in Victor Hugo's 'Notre Dame de Paris' (1831). The classic story of Quasimodo, the deaf, deformed, bell-ringing Hunchback of Notre Dame, and his hopeless love for a pretty Gypsy dancing girl, was an early epic. *Esmeralda* (1906) was directed by that rarity, a lady: Alice Guy. Henri Vorins and Denise Becker pantomimed the tale Goethe called 'the most detestable ever written' in ten terrible minutes. The plot was pirated around the world, in America by Vitagraph, *The Hunchback* (1909), and Selig, *Hugo the Hunchback* (1910), while the first production of that long-lived British emporium, Butcher's Films, was *The Love of a Hunchback* (1910). As with his transatlantic cousins, this humped hero followed in Quasimodo's pathetic footsteps by saving his unrequited beloved and dying with what passed for a brave smile on his face.

The following year the original hunchback became the first full-length monster in the movies. *Notre Dame de Paris* (1911) was filmed by Pathé in three parts. Quasimodo was played by Henri Krauss, Esmeralda by Stacia Napierkowska, a dancer who would become the first movie Queen of Atlantis.

For Quasimodo, there was only one transformation: from life to death. This is life's reality. Our escape clause is imagination, once into the fantasy of fable, now into the fantasy of film. When Beauty

Crustaceous Creatures: Spirit from *Night of the Demon* (Columbia 1957; *top left*) and Selenite from *A Trip to the Moon* (Méliès 1902; *centre left*).
Freak Show: *Horror of Malformed Men* (Toei 1969; *above right*), Victor Maddern in *Blood of the Vampire* (Eros 1958; *bottom left*) and Jane Adams in *House of Dracula* (Universal 1945; *below right*).

Ape Aped: *Balaoo the Demon Baboon* was made in France by Eclair in 1913, and in Hollywood by Twentieth Century-Fox in 1942. Fox called it *Dr Renault's Secret* and starred George Zucco as Dr Renault and J. Carrol Naish as his Secret (*opposite*).

Méliès' Monsters: Georges Méliès made monsters of many kinds, from bird-men of ancient Egypt (*below*) to an articulated Apocalyptic Horse (*The Merry Frolics of Satan* 1906; *bottom*).

kisses the Beast, we can actually see him change into the handsome Prince. In the movies our dreams come true; but so do our nightmares.

The magical metamorphosis of *Beauty and the Beast* was first filmed by Pathé as early as 1899. But such was the overwhelming welter of pantomimic confusion in French films of the Méliès era that when the London firm of Clarendon produced their *Beauty and the Beast* (1905), they advertised it as 'A real fairy story told as it should be told – No French cooks, no ballet girls!' Three years later Pathé remade it, crediting Madame Le Prince de Beaumont as author of 'the interesting story of a beautiful girl who is loved by a hideous animal'.

The other great early inspiration for French producers was Darwin. *The Doctor's Experiment* (1908) was a monkey-gland injection that made unsuspecting patients act like apes, while *The Monkey Man* (1908) was a gruesome preview of transplants to come.

'While a surgeon is trepanning his patient, an accident happens to the grey matter and the surgeon has it replaced by the brain of a monkey. After this the man performs all sorts of eccentric actions. The surgeon, having become very much interested in this curious case, leads his patient through the streets to the great pleasure of all believers in the Darwin theory.'

Feature-length treatment of the topic came with *Balaoo* (1913), which American distributors subtitled *The Demon Baboon*. Victorin Jasset directed it from a newspaper serial by Gaston Leroux. Darwin disciple Dr Coriolis transforms an enormous baboon into a half-humanized monster. Having terrorized the locals Balaoo takes to the trees and turns up in Switzerland. Here he becomes the tool of a poacher called Hubert. Ordered to abduct the doctor's daughter, Balaoo builds a trap. Hubert falls in and breaks both his legs, while the wounded Balaoo explains all in mime, then expires. Lucien Bataille played Balaoo 'so like a baboon that we forgot he really wasn't one,' wrote H.C. Judson.

Night Fright: William Castle's 'Emergo' brought Leona Anderson screaming out at Carolyn Craig in *House on Haunted Hill* (Allied Artists 1958; *opposite above*), ten years ahead of the Japanese apparition in *The Snake Girl and the Silverhaired Witch* (Daiei 1968; *left*).

Kiss of Death: Virginia North as Vulnavia smiles in the face of death, Vincent Price as Dr Anton Phibes in *The Abominable Dr Phibes* (American International 1971; *opposite below*). Embracing fearlessly *below* are two of William Castle's *Thirteen Ghosts* (Columbia 1960).

The Vengeance of Egypt (1912) was the first feature sold purely on the strength of its horror: 'A story in the Maupassant school, its object is horror, always a new horror.' This Gaumont film opened with no less a notable than Napoleon, digging up a mummy case. Lieutenant Girard steals the mummy's scarab ring and sends it to his sweetheart. When she puts it on she dreams of a mummy blinking its eyes and is promptly murdered by a burglar. An antiquary tries on the ring and dies of blotches on the arm. A toff buys it and gets shot; lovers find it and are killed in a plane crash. The uncanny catalogue only ends when an Egyptologist returns the ring to the mummy: its eyes glow again, presumably with satisfaction.

H.G.Wells' theory of evolution by vivisection, 'The Island of Dr Moreau' (1896), was thinly disguised by Eclipse as *The Island of Terror* (1913). Washed ashore somewhere in the Pacific is George Ramsey, a shipwrecked editor. His host, Dr Wagner, seems less hospitable when a stream of blood comes flowing under George's bedroom door. He discovers the doctor practising a grafting experiment upon a live black victim. The experiment fails and Wagner decides to try it on George. The editor escapes by raft, so Wagner, ever resourceful, substitutes his own assistant. In the struggle an oil lamp is overturned. Three victims push him into the flames and lock him in his blazing laboratory.

The terrible image of blood oozing under a locked door was repeated in *The Lunatics* (1913), Eclair's film of André de Lord's play, 'Le Système du Docteur Goudron et du Professeur Plume'. Henri Gouget and Monsieur Bahier played the mad characters based on Edgar Allan Poe's Dr Tarr and Professor Fether. Said trade critic George Blaisdell,

'It is a powerful story and a horrible one, yet fascinating in spite of its horror. Don't show it to your patrons without looking at it for yourself, for it is no food for infants or weaklings.' Said the advertising copywriter, 'Every scene a thrill – but the thrill of thrills, that terrifying thunderstorm with its awe-inspiring climax, stamps this feature as the greatest masterpiece of modern cinematography.' It was the first storm in horror movies; it would not be the last.

Brezard is dispatched to research an article on the Berneville Asylum, where Dr Maillard, the director, has developed a new way of treating psychopaths. Pretty Madame Brezard goes along for the ride. As they drive up to the old castle, a thunderstorm breaks. The inmates mutiny. Overpowering Dr Maillard, they hold him down as one lunatic raises a knife: 'to cure him quickly'. The Brezards' arrival interrupts the operation. Passing the knife to a colleague, the lunatic hurries into the director's office. 'His blanched face, glaring and staring eyes, and jerking motions cause the young couple great apprehension.' The 'director' describes his new cure for insanity. 'To their astonishment the chief step is cutting out an eye, and then, very carefully, the throat is to be sliced with a sharp knife!'

> 'Suddenly, a horrible and sickening rattle breaks up the interview. He rushes into the next room and returns a few minutes later, his hands covered with blood. For some little time strange beings have invaded the office. Their attitude is incomprehensible, their gestures wild. The sight of blood slowly oozing under the door awakens their murderous instincts, and they overpower Brezard. They prepare him for the operation. A wilder gust of wind blows the big window wide. The lunatics cower and this gives time for the keepers, now freed, to arrive with straight-jackets and master the madmen.'

The *Grand Guignol* of Paris, that theatre of horrors which had replaced the guillotine as a public entertainment, had arrived in the cinema – belatedly but brilliantly. The new director – of the film, not the asylum – was a student of Rodin, an actor with Rejane, and the first great French film-maker. Maurice Tourneur's brilliance with visuals was quickly lost to France. Eclair sent him to America to supervise their subsidiary studio. The horror film shifts with him.

Heads of Horror: Georges Méliès menaced by a monster skull (*left*). Peter Cushing eyes the remains of the Marquis de Sade in *The Skull* (Amicus 1965; *opposite*).

'DR. JEKYLL IS NOT HIMSELF'

In which James Cruze is Jekyll and Mr Hyde is somebody else, Uncle Carl makes his first monster, John Barrymore loses his Great Profile, and Mr Ogle's eyeballs leave Percy Darrell Standing.

The transformation of man into monster, for long years a fairy tale, for longer a legend, finally achieved physical manifestation in 1887. American theatregoers could scarce believe it when handsome Richard Mansfield, thirty-year-old matinee idol, shrank into a hideous dwarf before their very eyes. As noble Henry Jekyll, M.D., he had drunk a drug that released the suppressed side of his personality as Edward Hyde. Robert Louis Stevenson wrote 'Dr Jekyll and Mr Hyde' in 1885; two years later Thomas Russell Sullivan dramatized it for the stage. It was the first science-fiction interpretation of the folk-tales of old, a modern rationalization of ancient superstition. For twenty years Mansfield toured in the title roles, mystifying millions with his on-stage change. A more concentrated, less literary, more sensational version was written by Luella Forepaugh and George F. Fish in 1897. This, too, had a long life and reached Chicago in 1908, a year after Mansfield's death. In the audience was Colonel William Selig, proprietor of the Polyscope Company. For the rest of the week the actors spent their daylight hours in Selig's studio, giving birth to the American horror film. *Dr Jekyll and Mr Hyde* (1908) condensed the play's four acts so tightly into one single spool of film that it even included the curtain! This rose to reveal Dr Jekyll and Alice, the Vicar's daughter, vowing their love in the vicarage garden.

> 'Then comes the transformation of the moral and physical character of Dr Jekyll from the admirable gentleman and scholar to the ferocious brute of a maniac known as Mr Hyde. He is irresistibly addicted to a drink of his own mixture. It sets him wild and his other self reigns supreme. He attacks his sweetheart. Her father approaches and interferes. With fiendish glee and demon strength, Hyde kills the Vicar, disappears, and the next moment is seen as Dr Jekyll.'

The transformation scene was, of course, the play's great gimmick. Selig filmed it directly, recording the actor as he followed the formula of Forepaugh and Fish.

> 'Dr Jekyll writhes as though in physical pain; assumes crouching position; during this with one hand he pulls portion of the wig which is brought forward and falls in a tangled mass over his forehead and eyes.'

Despite super reviews ('the change is displayed with a dramatic ability almost beyond comprehension') the actor went unbilled. Anonymity was still accepted practice two years later, when Wrench released *The Duality of Man* (1910). In this variation Hyde indulges in high play in a pleasure garden, then makes off with the stakes.

> 'Detectives are hot on the trail when the criminal returns to his chambers and changes his identity. Hilda, the fiancée of the doctor, enters with her father, when again Hyde appears and murders him in the sight of the girl. The police enter, and the miscreant takes a fatal dose of poison.'

Nordisk's *Dr Jekyll and Mr Hyde* (1910) was the first version to name its star, Alwin Neuss. Director August Blom was called 'a sugar-coater of crime' for finding 'a very ingenious way of putting this drama before the young people and the various Boards of Censorship': 'The last scene shows Jekyll struggling with the nightmare in his chair, and, awakening in the presence of Maud, thanks God it was all a dream.' The reviewer added, 'We are inclined to think that Stevenson might just as well have done the same thing without hurting his story.' Already a new class of picturegoer – the middle class – was making its presence, and its predilections, felt.

All Change: Fredric March's not-so-easy switch from Jekyll to Hyde in *Dr Jekyll and Mr Hyde* (Paramount 1931).

Vampire Vamps: Theda Bara, the first vampire star, gave the world a new verb but no nightmares. More supernatural (indeed more super) is today's vampire star Ingrid Pitt, who played the colourful Carmilla in Hammer's *The Vampire Lovers* (1970; *opposite*). Alice Eis repeated her stage success in Kalem's *The Vampire* (1913; *left*), luring her dancing-partner Bert French into the next trance. Everybody danced in Roman Polanski's *Dance of the Vampires* (Filmways 1967; *below*), which caught filmgoers on the hop. Made as *Your Teeth in My Neck*, it was released in America as *The Fearless Vampire Killers*.

No such cop-outs for Lucius Henderson, who directed the Thanhouser *Dr Jekyll and Mr Hyde* (1911). James Cruze played Jekyll, and his wife, Marguerite Snow, his village sweetheart. Whether Alice, Hilda, or Maud we know not; subtitles simply call her 'the Minister's daughter'.

We see genial, white-locked Dr Jekyll sampling his steaming potion in his laboratory. He chokes, and sinks into his chair, head slumped on chest. A quick frame-cut and Mr Hyde raises his black-curled head. Brows beetle over popping eyeballs and fangs poke out at the corners of his mouth. His tail-coat is pretty shabby, too. Crooking his fingers and clawing the air, he scuttles off to attack his fiancée and strangle her father. In the end he wrecks his lab and drinks poison as a burly bobby barges down the door. The most startling aspect of the whole production was not disclosed for more than fifty years. In 1963 the octogenarian actor Harry Benham revealed that he, and not James Cruze, had played Mr Hyde! Historic stuff; but there is more. The next version of the Stevenson story would be the first horror film produced by a studio that would corner the genre, letting loose upon the world more monsters than any other source in the history of the cinema.

Carl Laemmle, a spry little German with twinkling blue eyes, was born in Lauphein in 1867. He was forty before he had enough cash behind him to throw over book-keeping for buying cinemas in Chicago. An independent spirit, he bucked Edison's Patents Company and was forced into production to feed his own cinemas. There was demoniac humour in his choice of symbol: his Independent Motion Picture Company contracted neatly into Imp. He bedevilled the Trust so expertly that in 1912 he combined Imp and other independents into the Universal Film Manufacturing Company, and in 1915 opened Universal City, a great studio built on the 230-acre Taylor Ranch in Lankershim, Los Angeles.

Universal's big name was King Baggot: sometimes it was even bigger, as nobody, not even he, seemed quite sure whether to spell it with a second 't'. Lured by Laemmle in 1910 upon the sudden folding of a seemingly secure stage tour, Baggot's weekly one-reelers won him early international stardom. He was the first 'character star' in cinema: a wizard of the makeup box. In one memorable movie, *Shadows* (1914), he played every

Hyde's Hide: Christopher Lee in *I, Monster* (Amicus 1970).

character in the story, all ten of them. Meanwhile, as a warm-up, he concentrated on but two: *Dr Jekyll and Mr Hyde* (1913). With crêpe hair and greasepaint 'as the hideous Hyde he brings shudders aplenty'. More than ever before, there was help from the camera. 'We get the real dissolving view as the drug begins to manifest its influence, in the place of the crude facial manipulations employed on the stage.'

Simultaneously the American studios of Charles Urban's Kinemacolor Company released their version of *Dr Jekyll and Mr Hyde* (1913), the first horror film photographed in colour. The system required double-speed projectors fitted with revolving red-green filters; thus distribution of the film was such that even trade-paper reviewers were unable to catch it.

Trick photography had raised movie metamorphoses beyond the capabilities of theatrical mechanics, but the technique had changed little from Méliès' methods. A jump cut, or the slightly more sophisticated dissolve, was considered enough. Henry McRae, a Canadian director who would outlast even Laemmle in the service of Universal, was content with a quick dissolve to convert Watuma, a white-hating, half-caste Navajo, into a live wolf. *The Werewolf* (1913) was the first film to illustrate the legend of the lycanthrope and is still the only one to go to the American Indian original.

The first film truly to transform man into beast by blending several stages of makeup through a series of dissolves, was Thanhouser's *The Miser's Conversion* (1914). Sidney Bracy played the 75-year-old miser obsessed by Darwin's theory. He offers his daughter to the Maharajah of Lahaif in return for rejuvenation. Before an audience, seated in a chair wired to a pulsimeter, Bracy is dosed with elixir. 'The wrinkles leave his brow, his cheeks fill out, his hair changes colour, and he is transformed into a man of forty.' When the Maharajah isn't looking, Bracy grabs the bottle and swallows the lot. 'Immediately he is changed into an ape! It is the most lifelike ape that ever walked on to a studio stage, and you'll marvel, gasp, and exclaim at the transformation!'

John Barrymore, sweet prince of Broadway's royal family, was thirty-eight. As handsome Henry in Paramount's *Dr Jekyll and Mr Hyde* (1920) he looked eighteen years younger. Yet when he quaffed his concoction he crabbed and contorted into a grinning thing of ancient evil. He did it before your very eyes, following the famous feat of

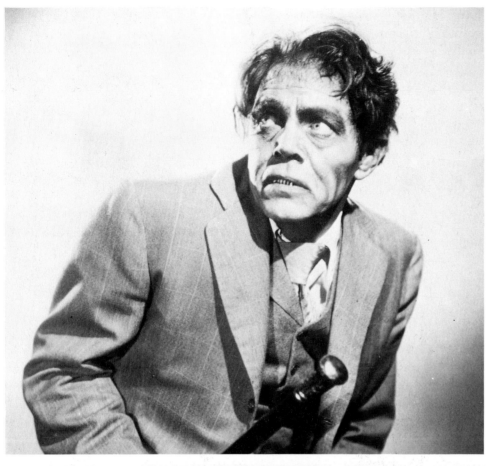

Hyde and Shriek: Monster movies' most popular double act is *Dr Jekyll and Mr Hyde*. James Cruze and Harry Benham played the double-exposed duo in this publicity still from 1912 (Thanhouser: *opposite left*). 1920 saw a double-header: John Barrymore (seen with Louis Wolheim in the Paramount picture; *opposite below*) and Sheldon Lewis (seen with Pearl White in the 1915 Pathé serial *The Exploits of Elaine*; *opposite right*). Fredric March won an Oscar for Henry-and-Edward in Paramount's 1931 version (Holmes Herbert is at the revolver), while twenty years later Louis Hayward played the schizophrenic *Son of Dr Jekyll* (Columbia 1951; *left*) in makeup by Clay Campbell.

Richard Mansfield but under the cold-eyed closeup of the camera. Only then came the trickery: a shot of Jekyll's fingers dissolving into bony talons, then director John S. Robertson cut back to show Hyde's face in full, foul makeup. The concept of the character was horribly new: instead of hairy ape, this Hyde is a spider. Under his high hat his head comes to a point; when he walks he scuttles on crooked legs; his hands, so elongated he has trouble turning his key, are like outsize arachnids. And when Jekyll sleeps, 'in his hours off guard, outraged nature took her hideous revenge and out of the black abyss of torment sent upon him the creeping horror that was his other self'. A phantom spider of monstrous size crawls into his bedroom, up on to his covers, and melts into his body. Jekyll wakes as Hyde.

Clara Beranger's screenplay extended the original and doubled the 'romantic interest'. Martha Mansfield played Millicent, daughter of cynical Sir George Carewe and the chocolate-box innocent whom Jekyll loves. Sultry Nita Naldi was Miss Gina, 'the famous H'Italian dancer' with whom Hyde shacks up at No. 9 Barnesbury Road, Soho. The sapping of Gina's earthy health into shadow-eyed pallor between subtly slow fades adds an uncomfortable new dimension to man's baser nature. There is much of Wilde's Dorian in this beautiful Henry, and of W.T.Stead's London under his perverted Hyde.

This splendid film was a triumph for actor ('pure motion-picture pantomime on as high a level as has ever been attained by anyone') and director, a claim which can be indisputably proved: the Paramount picture had its own *doppelgänger*. Released simultaneously with Jesse L. Lasky's sumptuous super was a poverty-row piece of the same name. Thanks to a quirk of copyright an ex-exhibitor was able to rush through a carbon copy and found a fortune that would ultimately exceed even that of Lasky's. Louis B. Mayer set his *Dr Jekyll and Mr Hyde* (1920) in modern dress. This not only put the production apart from Paramount's just in case a suit should ensue, it also saved the cost of costumes. For his double star Mayer chose Sheldon Lewis, a name known mainly to serial fans. A shrewd move, for not only did Mayer gain a star of sorts, but Lewis brought along his 'Clutching Hand' kit at no extra charge. (He had played that monstrous menace in *The Exploits of Elaine*, 1915.)

The two films tell the story of Cinema 1920 – the one, beautifully tailored for the top box-office star of his time, told with all the expertise of the contemporary American movie; the other relying entirely on flatly filmed histrionics, hastily pasted together with high-flown, quasi-religious subtitles. The style of direction (which was anonymous), acting, and camera-trickery of the latter is exactly that of the James Cruze film of 1912: a one-reeler blown to five.

Lewis' Jekyll metamorphoses the easy way: a swig at a test-tube, a cut-away to a butler brushing his hat, and a cut-back to Hyde, crouching and clutching away. 'An Apostle of Hell!' shrieks a horrified subtitle. Proceeding to 'a squalid tenement district' Hyde indulges in 'crimes of his demon nature': he leaps out at a passing female and snatches her handbag. Hyde lurks in his laboratory as fiancée Bernice comes a-calling. 'Dr Jekyll is not himself,' warns the butler. Nabbed by Chief Barnes of the local precinct, Hyde is given the Third Degree. Strapped in the electric chair he dissolves to Jekyll dozing in his armchair. It was all a dream! 'I believe in God!' he cries, 'I have a soul – and I shall have *you*!' he adds, as Bernice bears him off to the opera.

Magic, myth, madness, metamorphosis. One more M came from Edison. He had made the movies; now he made a monster.

'Oh! No mortal could support the horror of that countenance!' The words of Victor Frankenstein, the Modern Prometheus of Mary Wollstonecraft Shelley's novel of 1816, must have found echo in many an exhibitor's exclamation as he opened his Edison envelope on the morning of 15 March 1910. For from the coloured cover of The Kinetogram, No. 4, Vol. 2, snarled 'Scene from *Frankenstein*, Film No. 6604': Charles Ogle.

'A giant in stature, Mr Ogle attracts instant attention whenever he appears on the screen, and from that moment never fails to hold it.' So wrote Edison's publicist, adding that Ogle in action 'has a power that is not easily forgotten'. Nor was his monstrous makeup. The theatrical tradition of the actor creating his own makeup had carried over into the movies, and Ogle's vision of the man-made monster came closer to Mrs Shelley's description than any other the screen has since seen. Only Ogle's eyeballs with their darkly distinctive pupils defied makeup and strayed from the watery original.

The film began in the Frankenstein home as the young student bade farewell to his father and sweetheart, then cut to his room at college where he sat 'absorbed in the mysteries of life and death'.

'He is convinced that he has found a way to create

Under the Hyde: Handsome Henry Jekyll was Spencer Tracy (seen with Ingrid Bergman, MGM 1941; *above*).

Oscar Hyde: Fredric March in *Dr Jekyll and Mr Hyde* (Paramount 1931; *opposite*).

the most perfect human being the world has ever seen. To Frankenstein's horror, instead of creating a marvel of physical beauty and grace, there is unfolded before his eyes an awful, ghastly, abhorrent monster.'

An aside by the synopsist now gives us a small hint of the cinematic quality of the creation scene. 'The formation of the hideous creature from the blazing chemicals of the huge cauldron in Frankenstein's laboratory is perhaps the most weird and fascinating scene ever shown in a moving picture.'

The horror piles up. Frankenstein rushes from the room, 'only to have the misshapen monster peer at him through the curtains of his bed. He falls fainting to the floor.' He returns home a broken man, but quickly recovers under the loving care of his sweetheart. This, moralizes the synopsist, 'brings out the fact that the creation of the monster was only possible because he had allowed his mind to be overcome by evil and unnatural thoughts.' Unable to live apart from his creator, the Monster returns on his wedding night and enters the bride's chamber. The film cuts to Frankenstein as he reacts to the sound of her scream. The girl rushes in and faints at his feet. The Monster is close behind; he overpowers Frankenstein and leaves. The final scene, claimed Edison, brought out the moral point 'that when love for his bride shall have attained full strength, it will have such an effect upon his mind that the monster cannot exist'.

'The monster enters the room, stands before a large mirror, and holds out his arms entreatingly. Gradually the real monster fades away leaving only the real image in the mirror. A moment later Frankenstein himself enters. As he stands directly before the mirror we are amazed to see the image of the monster reflected instead of Frankenstein's own. Gradually, however, under the effects of love and his better nature, the monster's image fades and Frankenstein sees himself in his young manhood in the mirror. His bride joins him and the film ends with their embrace.'

Frankenstein ran to 975 feet in America, but only 967 feet in England. Was it the first horror film to be censored – or were the English simply better at counting?

Five years later the Ocean Film Corporation proudly announced their first five-reel feature, *Life Without Soul* (1915).

'The action is laid in the semi-tropics of Florida, the desert wastes of Arizona, the awe-inspiring mountainous regions of interior Georgia, the canyons of Colorado, the decks of a three-masted schooner, an ocean-going liner, and the parlors of refined New York.'

Exhibitors were surprised to discover that the film was actually *Frankenstein* again, as adapted by Jesse J. Goldburg, Vice-President and General Manager, and directed by Colonel Joseph W. Smiley, Preceptor of Directors. Percy Darrell Standing, an English actor, played 'the Creation':

'His embodiment of the man without a soul adequately conveys the author's intent. He is awe-inspiring, but never grotesque, and indicates the gradual unfolding of the creature's senses and understanding with convincing skill. At times, he actually awakens sympathy for the monster's condition, cut off as he is from all human companionship.'

Words which would be used of another English actor in a later version. But despite Standing's performance and the elaborately modernized script, the film failed, and it was taken over by the Raver Film Corporation. Mr Raver himself injected 'scientific scenes showing the blood coursing through the veins, the conjugation of cells, and the reproduction of life in the fish world'. Claimed he, 'In its new form, *Life Without Soul*, besides its entertaining value, also has an educational

worth.' Nobody went to his version, either.

'A sort of psychic Frankenstein' was the publicist's description of the Thought Monster, a creature conjured up by The Grand Master of the Black Order in the ultimate episode of *The Mysteries of Myra* (1916), a serial advertised as 'Fifteen Chapters of Science Versus the Supernatural'.

'This Monster is a huge and powerful creature. But his disposition is sort of like a child, in that he is easily distracted from his purpose. He starts to smash up things in the laboratory and to kill Myra. He sees his reflection in the mirror and forgets what he is after.'

Also cast in Frankenstein's monster mould was Q the Automaton, mechanical henchman of the villain in the Harry Houdini serial, *The Master Mystery* (1918).

'The creature is of immense size and fearsome aspect. It can batter down doors at a single strike, and barricades of furniture against them are of no avail against its immense strength. Its movements are ponderous and jerky, but always emphatic, and in spite of its grotesque appearance, the creature is never ridiculous.'

Purporting to be 'an automatic robot containing a human brain taken from a dying man and revivified by a mad genius', inside Q was actually actor Floyd Buckley. Meanwhile, in the European cradle of horrible legends, a human Frankenstein had unleashed a monster the like of which the world had scarcely dreamed.

Hyde and Find: *Abbott and Costello Meet Dr Jekyll and Mr Hyde* (Universal 1953; *above*); Peter Cushing catches Christopher Lee on the turn (Amicus 1970; *above right*); March sees his alter ego (Paramount 1931; *below right*).

THE CLAY MAN COMETH -
AND COMETH BACK

**In which the Student of Prague makes a Bargain with Satan,
Herr Wegener makes a Golem, Dr Caligari makes a Cabinet,
and Rotwang makes a Robot.**

The German nightmare would begin, in reality, in the summer of 1914. As a foretaste, that favourite literary myth of the *doppelgänger* – a vision of oneself, the sight of which foretells death – had appeared on screen as early as 1909. *The Haunted Man* was produced by Düskes. 'Wherever he goes the same ghostly figure (apparent to none but himself) rises up with horrid imitations of his own actions.' Dogged by his remorseless spook, the haunted man flies to his lodgings where he is promptly doused by his landlady. A drier fate awaited Balduin, the doubled one of *A Bargain With Satan* (1913). This adaptation of Alfred de Musset's poem was publicized as 'a splendid modern allegory of the supernatural, crowded with meaning and mysticism. Better than Faust and Dr Jekyll and Mr Hyde put together!'

Balduin, penniless student of Prague, is visited by the shrivelled Dr Scapinelli, who offers him 100,000 gold pieces in return for permission to take whatever he wishes. Balduin takes the cash and Scapinelli takes Balduin's reflection, for Scapinelli is Satan and the reflection Balduin's soul. Now he is rich enough to woo a Countess. The lady, however, is engaged to Baron Waldis, who challenges his upstart rival to a duel. Balduin promises the Countess that he will not kill the Baron, then meets his victorious reflection, derisively wiping gory sword on cloak. The double pursues him; Balduin pulls a gun and fires. The double vanishes, and Balduin falls dead, blood gushing from his side.

A world success, there was praise for Danish director Stellan Rye, cameraman Guido Seeber ('As an example of ingenious double photography it will strike amazement into the uninitiated'), and the stage star from the Max Reinhardt theatre making a double debut in films. 'Perhaps the most remarkable feature of the film is the superb performance of Herr Paul Wegener. In his last fantastic flight from the spectre he conveys an expression of terror which is irresistibly communicated to the spectator.'

They made the film on location in Prague, where Wegener was much taken by the ancient Ghetto. One legend the old Jews told so intrigued him that he used it as the basis of his next picture. In *Der Golem* (1914) Wegener not only produced, co-wrote, and co-directed, he also played that stalking statue which his American distributors dubbed *The Monster of Fate*. Clad in clay-caked cloth, a thick wig on his head, the moon-faced Teuton stomped through the streets, smashing his way through glass doors and panicking the populace in his love-crazed pursuit of an antique dealer's daughter. The old man had bought the Golem from excavators who thought it was a statue. The dealer recognized it as the legendary clay-man created by a sixteenth-century Rabbi to protect his persecuted people from an evil Emperor. Brought back to life by a magic charm, the Golem reverts to stone when the girl snatches the charm from its chest. Falling from a tower it is broken on the cobblestones below.

The film itself met an equally shattering end. War was declared, preventing its export to England. It arrived in America somewhat belatedly and opened the week the US declared war. A key work in the monster genre, its influence was confined to its own country, where war had an unusual side-effect. German cinema, no longer dominated by America, grew fantastically. New studios were built to cope with the public's demand for escape and movies went back indoors, where it was safe from bombs. Under the bright lights native production bloomed. Cinema abandoned the reality of Lumière's open air and returned to first base: Méliès. To the artificially-created film was added the other Méliès line: fantasy.

Paul Wegener became the first film-maker since Méliès to specialize in the supernatural. From his

Pillar of Society: *The Golem* (Union 1920). Paul Wegener, monster and director.

Famulus, Loew's assistant, discovers the old man's daughter in bed with the Junker. The jealous youth orders the Golem to kill. All hell breaks loose. The clay man punches through the girl's door, throws her lover from a tower, grabs up a blazing log. Soon the whole cramped Ghetto is ablaze as the Golem drags the swooning girl away and drapes her over an accommodatingly-curved rock. He crashes open the great gates: children flee screaming. One little girl stands and smiles. She offers him her apple. The Golem picks her up. She plays with his amulet, takes out the charm: he stiffens, falls, a statue of stone.

Wegener's way with cinema attracted other intellectuals from the arts. A discharged lieutenant tried his hand at scenario writing whilst convalescing from war wounds. The result, *Hilde Warren und der Tod* (1917), inspired Fritz Lang to forsake his pre-war career as a painter and take up films. Director Joe May's wife Mia played Hilde Warren, and Lang himself played Tod (Death): a suitably supernatural beginning for a cinematic career that would stretch to the sixties.

The end of the war saw Lang a scenario editor, 1919 a director. Too busy to take on a horror story he had accepted from two young pacifist poets, Lang passed the script to Robert Wiene, but not before he had added two framing scenes. These, complained Hans Janowitz and Carl Meyer, took their tale of insanity out of reality and into explicable illusion. Nevertheless, *The Cabinet of Dr Caligari* (1919) is still not only a great horror film, it is a classic of cinema.

'Ladies and gentlemen. You are about to see what is without a doubt the strangest motion picture ever made. It may add to your appreciation if you know something of the aims of the producers. They believed that the screen could be made something more than a mere medium for the exact photographic reproduction of conventional stories. They considered that motion pictures could be made to reflect the newest and most interesting development in modern art, and that, in so doing, produce sensations and emotions in an audience that have hitherto been impossible. They have told a thrilling and fantastic story in somewhat the same manner in which an artist transfers his own emotions upon canvas – in vivid and unusual strokes of colour and composition. To do this they have made the backgrounds an important part of the story. In every scene there is a special setting made and painted by hand [designed by Hermann Warm, Walter Reimann and Walter Röhrig, painters from *Der Sturm* group in Berlin], which fits the mood of the action that is taking place. You will see Cesare, the sleep-walker, floating down the street that seems to have been ripped from some nightmare – a street of misshapen houses with brooding windows, streaked by dagger strokes of light and darkened by blots of shadow – and you will immediately feel the terror in the movements of that floating grotesque.'

This was how the British distributors introduced the film in 1922, by which time hostilities had cooled sufficiently for it to be billed, cautiously, as 'Europe's Greatest Contribution to the Motion Picture Art'. German publicists put it more simply: 'You Must Become Caligari!'

'In Holstenwall where I was born': Francis tells the tale in flashback, of a village fair and a hypnotist: 'Step up! Step up! See Cesare the Somnambulist! Cesare who has slept for twenty-five years and

Wax Wonders: Waxwork shows have been scaring up a fortune since the pre-cinema days of Madame Tussaud and her Chamber of Horrors. Paul Leni's *Waxworks* (Neptune 1924; *opposite left*) brought to life Emil Jannings as Haroun-al-Raschid, Conrad Veidt as Ivan the Terrible, and Werner Krauss as Jack the Ripper. The sequence featuring Rinaldo Rinaldini was not finally included. Michael Curtiz made real actors stand in for the models in *Mystery of the Wax Museum* (Warner 1933; *opposite right*); the Technicolor lights melted the originals.

Doctor's Orders: The influence of *The Cabinet of Dr Caligari* (Decla 1919; *below left*) can be seen in Jean Hersholt's gloves in *The Cat Creeps* (Universal 1930; *left*) and the coffin in *Dance of the Vampires* (Filmways 1967; *below*).

Shadow Shudder: The Germans were so fond of shadows that they made a film about them, *Warning Shadows* (Pan 1923), a year after Schreck's shadow crept in *Nosferatu* (*above*). The shadow of Vincent Price frightened Phyllis Kirk in *House of Wax* (Warner 1953; *opposite above*), a three-dimensional remake of *Mystery of the Wax Museum*. Shadows also struck home a point in Polanski's *Dance of the Vampires* (Filmways 1967; *opposite below*).

'I am Dracula. I bid you Welcome.': Max Schreck was Dracula but had to be called Graf Orlok to fool Bram Stoker's widow. F.W.Murnau's dodge failed, but his film did not. *Nosferatu* (Prana 1922; *above left*) remains a frightening thrill unequalled even by Tod Browning's *Dracula* (Universal 1931; *left*), with Bela Lugosi as the legal, lethal Count.

Veidt Fright: Conrad Veidt was the first great figure of fright in cinema. Following in the sturdier footsteps of Paul Wegener he created a unique creature in Cesare the skeletal Somnambulist, whose awakening was an eye-opener in *The Cabinet of Dr Caligari* (Decla 1919: *opposite right*). In *Waxworks* (Neptune 1924; *opposite left*) he was mad Ivan the Terrible, who went even madder trying to stop an hour-glass from emptying away his life. In Robert Wiene's *The Hands of Orlac* (Pan 1924; *top*) he was a concert pianist on to whose severed stumps were grafted the hands of a murderer. Peter Lorre played the part in Karl Freund's version, shown in America as *Mad Love* (MGM 1935; *right*) and Mel Ferrer did it again for Edmond T. Greville (Pendennis 1960; *above*).

is about to awake!' At a command from Caligari (Werner Krauss in Mutt and Jeff gloves: three stripes on each to match his hair), Cesare (Conrad Veidt at his most skeletal in skin-tight leotards) opens his black-lidded eyes and cat-foots forth from his coffin. It is a moment of death into life that still chills. 'Cesare knows all secrets – ask him to look into your future!' Francis' frail friend asks, 'How long shall I live?' And Cesare answers, 'Until dawn!' The awful prediction comes true: Cesare murders him. Commanded to kill Jane Olsen (Lil Dagover, all mascara and white drapery) Cesare comes creeping through her window, knife at the ready. Her beauty gives him pause – she wakes – he snarls – she screams – they struggle – she swoons – he bears her off over the crooked roofs, a pack of outraged villagers at his heels. A classic sequence, classically constructed; as well made as any made today.

Francis exposes Dr Sonnow, head of the local lunatic asylum, as Caligari, insanely obsessed by exploits of an eleventh-century mountebank – but then Francis is exposed as a lunatic himself! This was the twist, added by Lang to 'explain' the unrealistic decor, that so upset Hans Janowitz. Even so the film was successful enough to create a whole new school of cinema, Expressionism. Immediately Janowitz was given *Dr Jekyll and Mr Hyde* to adapt for the newest star of German horror, Conrad Veidt (another Reinhardt refugee). This film was another inexpensive piece. To avoid possible royalties it called its doubled hero Dr Warren and Mr O'Connor and itself *Der Januskopf* (1920). The fine physician who turned into a Whitechapel murderer under the influence of a statue of Janus, was photographed by Karl Freund and directed by F.W.Murnau.

Friedrich Wilhelm Murnau, whose real name was Plumpe, was yet another Reinhardt-trained man. His success at pirating Stevenson now led him to another late English novelist, and from Bram Stoker's 'Dracula' (1897) he evolved *Nosferatu* (1922). He subtitled it *Eine Symphonie des Grauens* (A Symphony of Shudders). He changed the characters' names: hero Harker became Hutter; his wife Nina, Ellen; Lucy Westenra became Annie Harding; Renfield, Knock; and Count Dracula, Graf Orlok. He changed London to Bremen and put the clock back to 1838. All this, and still the widow sued. Mrs Stoker won her case and all copies of the film were destroyed; or so the order went. In 1930 there turned up a talkie called *Die Zwölfte Stunde* (The Twelfth Hour), concerning a vampire called Fürst Wollkoff. He was Orlok-Dracula with a music-and-effects track added. Whatever man's law may decree, a vampire cannot die – as long as a film duper shall live. *Nosferatu* is the classic example of art saved from destruction by piracy.

Hutter arrives at a crumbling castle after a frightening ride in a high-speed coach drawn by shrouded horses. His hook-nosed host, skull-capped and skeletal, comes only by night. Creeping into his guest's room, Orlok is about to bite him when Ellen Hutter, in distant Bremen, wakes screaming from her sleep. This telepathic miracle interrupts the vampire, who packs his coffin and heads for the docks. Once aboard the *Empusa* the feast is on: soon only the mate and the captain are left alive. The mate chops open Orlok's crate – rats come swarming out. From his coffin Orlok swings upright, stare-eyed and smiling, as if on some horrid hinge. The mate plunges overboard and the captain ties himself to the wheel as the vampire creeps forth. The dead ship sails into harbour. Orlok scuttles away, his coffin tucked underneath his arm. Soon funerals fill the streets. Orlok stares in at Ellen's window. She welcomes him, embraces him, deceiving him to linger. Dawn warms the sky and as the sun strikes him, the vampire dissolves: a puff of smoke, and then that too is gone.

Thin Max Schreck played the bony blood-sucker in Spock-ears and eagle-claws. A skin wig made him look much older than his forty-three years. Schreck died in 1936, a veteran of more than fifty films: all but this forgotten. He was the first and foulest vampire in the movies.

Nosferatu used real settings, selected, framed, and lit with care. The interplay of light and shade replaced Caligari's black paint: in the horror film Expressionism had found its form. Unrealistic set design rolled on. Paul Leni, who had created great stage settings for Reinhardt, directed *Waxworks* (1924). An omnibus film following the Fritz Lang formula from *Destiny* (1921), it allowed Leni's designing mind to run wild. Opening in a crazy carnival, Wilhelm Dieterle (later William, the director) played a starving poet hired to create tales around the models in a waxworks show. In his fantasies Emil Jannings is Haroun-al-Raschid, bulbous lecher; Conrad Veidt is Ivan the Terrible, maniacal torturer; Werner Krauss is Jack the Ripper, relentless pursuer. Veidt's wrought performance as the insane Ivan is still one of the most compellingly disturbing in all cinema. He went on to play the obsessed amputee of *The Hands of Orlac* (1924), from a French science-fiction prediction of transplant surgery. Maurice Renard's popular novel was given much medieval trappery, as may have been expected from director Robert Wiene, who had helped create Caligarism five years before. Paul Orlac is a concert pianist whose hands are crushed in a crash. A surgeon sews on those of a murderer (Fritz Kortner), and sensitive Paul feels a subsequent urge. The consequent killings are, however, nothing more than a foul plot to drive the mended man mad. Strictly supernatural, however, was the remake of *The Student of Prague* (1926), in which Veidt sold his soul to Satan: Werner Krauss in top-hat, tail-coat and gamp.

Meanwhile, Fritz Lang had spent more than a year and most of UFA's money on *Metropolis* (1926), a symbolic prediction of the year 2000. Rudolph Klein-Rogge played Rotwang, a madly medieval scientist who single-handedly (literally: his right hand was a black-gloved claw) created a robotrix in the image of a 'girl of the people'. This *doppelgänger* was played both in flesh and steel sheathing by a student spotted in an amateur play. Brigitte Helm acquitted herself erotically enough to play later both Alraune, the man-created woman of *A Daughter of Destiny* (1928), and Antinea, queen of Atlantis; the former twice.

Metropolis, essentially a science-fiction spectacular, also sought to reform the boss-worker relationship: a fantasy on two levels. However, Lang put enough cracked magic into his laboratory sequences to spark off monsters unborn. The undoubted prototype for Frankenstein's, and every other mad movie doctor's lab, it added the new futurism to the old Expressionism. Alchemy both ancient and ultra-modern came together in the contrast of flashing light and frightening shadow. And as Lang looked into tomorrow and saw some of yesterday, Murnau looked back and found *Faust* (1926). From that old, much-filmed legend Murnau and Freund conjured cinema's definitive devil: Emil Jannings, horned and huge, flies through the night, enfolding a whole rolling town in the blackness of his cloak. This unequalled sequence, together with Lang's epic vision, makes 1926 the climax to an incredibly creative decade: a heritage of horror that was Germany's silent gift to the cinema.

Sleep Walkers: Conrad Veidt drags over Lil Dagover in *The Cabinet of Dr Caligari* (Decla 1919).

The Unholy Three (1925) were Echo (Chaney), a ventriloquist, Hercules, a strong man, and Tweedledee, a midget. Seeking to expand their extra-curricular activity of picking the pockets of circus customers, the incredible partnership sets up shop with Echo in charge as 'the Little Lady who Sells Parrots'. Their scheme is mind-blowing. Echo, beaded and bombazined, sells a talking parrot to a rich client. When the client complains that the bird no longer talks (it never did; Echo was ventriloquizing, of course), the Little Lady comes a-calling. She brings along her baby, who promptly clambers from his pram to stuff any spare jewellery down his diaper (the midget in disguise, you see). By way of a climax, Browning introduces a giant gorilla. 'Startling and original', exclaimed one reviewer.

Delighted with his *Hunchback* profits, Carl Laemmle determined to do the whole exercise again. He looked to France for another epic and found in Gaston Leroux's 1908 novel everything he could hope for: a magnificent set to build that would rival Notre Dame, and a horrible monster to create that would outdo Quasimodo. *The Phantom of the Opera* (1925) brought Lon Chaney hurrying back home to Universal.

'Sanctuary of song lovers. The Paris Opera House, rising nobly over medieval torture chambers, hidden dungeons long forgotten. One night each year all Paris mingled, forgetful of caste, at the merry, mad Bal Masqué de l'Opéra. In the midst of the revelry strode a spectral figure robed in red.'

This fearsome figure in crimson cloak and scarlet skull – Poe's 'Red Death' in two-tone Technicolor – is the Phantom. Erik, a born freak, lives only for music. Periodically he slinks from the shadows to whisper unseen tuition to Christine the chorus girl. When the directors of the Opera spoil her chance to deputize for a diva, the Phantom is angry. He sends a giant crystal chandelier crashing into the audience. In black cloak and white mask he emerges from a mirror to conduct Christine through cobwebby catacombs and across an underground lake to his lair. The Phantom sits at an organ and plays 'Don Juan Triumphant', his own composition (first heard four years later when David Broekman and Max Hayman added it to the film for a synchronized reissue). What follows is classic, of horror cinema and of cinema itself. Christine (Mary Philbin), unable to resist the fascination of fear, unmasks the Phantom.

Chaney's makeup had been kept secret by the studio during the shooting. When it was eventually revealed, quite late in the film, it was by as cunningly contrived a sequence of shots as was ever devised in the history of montage. Women screamed and strong men fainted. By careful placement of characters and camera, Rupert Julian doubles the shock. The first is for us: Christine is behind Chaney and cannot see his face. The second is for her when Chaney turns. Thus, through her shock, his face shocks us again.

'Feast your eyes, gloat your soul, on my accursed ugliness!' We can scarce do otherwise as Julian's camera cuts closeups, longshots, distorted shots, together into a film thrill unequalled until James Whale's revelation of his Frankenstein Monster. This was the original unmasking sequence in horror movies, and of a hundred seen since is still the best. It thrilled again when Universal spliced it into their 1951 mystery, *Hollywood Story*. Yet two full remakes and a third reconstruction for Chaney's biography, all in colour, have failed to catch that awful shock.

Chaney created a makeup intended to suggest a living skull. He designed a device that, inserted into his nose, tilted the tip and spread open his nostrils. Another device drew his mouth back at the corners, prongs attached to protruding false teeth. Inside his mouth, circles of celluloid accentuated his cheekbones, and on top of his head was a domed wig of skin, stranded with lank hair.

The film ended with a wild chase and an in-joke: pursued by a torch-bearing mob the Phantom drives his frantic coach past Notre Dame. Universal's most expensive production was banned in Britain, not because of its horrors, but from Parliamentary outrage. An over-enthusiastic publicist persuaded His Majesty's soldiery to escort the precious print from Southampton to Wardour Street!

British sensitivity changed the title of the next Chaney and Browning venture: *London After Midnight* (1927) became *The Hypnotist* in England. It was the first true American vampire movie despite the twist in its tail. Authentic vampire trappings abounded: twin punctures in the jugular, a hickory stick staked through the heart, pallid and dark-eyed lovelies at the window. Before the Browning version, Hollywood vampires had been pallid and dark-eyed lovelies of the Theda Bara breed: sucking their men dry but not of blood. Chaney had his

Phantom Poster: Claude Rains as *The Phantom of the Opera* (Universal 1943).

Claude Rains
as The Phantom

Lugosi Poster: *The Mystery of the Mary Celeste* (Hammer 1936; *opposite*).

Haunting Refrain: Music and monsters went well together, even in the silent cinema. *The Phantom of the Opera* (Universal 1925; *bottom right*) did the rounds with a special score for pit orchestra or pianist. Later versions had the music built in. In 1943 Susanna Foster sang 'The Melody of the Bells' to Claude Rains (*below*) and in 1962 Hammer's Herbert Lom serenaded with 'Saint Joan' (*bottom*).

expected unmasking scene, but in reverse. Swiftly divesting himself of frizzy fright-wig and fangs, the hideous vampire uncrooked to stand revealed as upright Inspector Burke of Scotland Yard, horn-rims and all! Outside the requisites of plot payoff, the make-up took a little longer: sharpened dentures made it painful for Chaney to speak, and wire loops in his eye-sockets were tightened before takes to bulge his eyes. The denouement was not, it appears, a cop-out. Claimed Browning:

> 'Mystery stories are tricky, for if they are too gruesome or horrible, if they exceed the average imagination by too much, the audience will laugh. *London After Midnight* is an example of how to get people to accept ghosts and other supernatural spirits by letting them turn out to be the machinations of a detective. Thereby the audience is not asked to believe the horrible impossible, but the horrible possible, and plausibility increased, rather than lessened, the thrills and chills.'

Within three years both Browning and his audience would have matured enough to accept the genuine vampire.

Carl Laemmle now sought a suitable follow-through to Chaney's Hunchback and Phantom. Looking to French literature again he discovered Victor Hugo's *The Man Who Laughs* (1928). This time MGM refused to let Chaney go. Undaunted, Laemmle turned to his native land and brought over the one other star who had carved a corner in macabre characters. Conrad Veidt made Gwymplaine, the disfigured heir with the perpetual grin, a monstrous Pagliacci. His hideous laugh whilst under torture in the Iron Maiden was too much for the box office to bear. Veidt's cadaverous character made the skin crawl without the redeeming humanity inherent in even Chaney's most horrible creations.

The star of the most sensational American silent film of them all was less than human, less even than animal. It was a toy, a thing of rubbery stuff moulded around a jointed wire skeleton, all of twelve inches high. But when shown on the cinema screen, it became a monstrous brontosaurus that made Tower Bridge come falling down. The fair lady was Bessie Love, a box-office attraction not found in Sir Arthur Conan Doyle's original novel of *The Lost World* (1925).

Wallace Beery played Professor Challenger, leader of an expedition up the Amazon to find prehistoric life. Among the flora and fauna was Bull Montana, the well-known apeman. This time he was in the full, hirsute suit, as created by First National's wizard of the whiskers, Cecil Holland. Acting and direction (Harry O. Hoyt) were no great shakes, but the camerawork and effects were the best the Hollywood movie had yet produced. A team of three photographed: Arthur Edeson, Fred Jackman and Homer Scott used masking and double-exposure to combine men with models that had to be shot in stop-motion, two frames at a time.

The man behind the models was an ex-cartoonist from Oakland named Willis O'Brien. He became the special effects king of Hollywood horrors and as such finally won an Academy Award in 1949 (for, curiously, his worst work, *Mighty Joe Young*.) Yet always his horror was diluted by the light touch inherited from his previous profession. It showed in his first film, *The Dinosaur and the Baboon* (1917). This told the 500-foot tale of Stonejaw Steve and Theophilus Ivoryhead who try to catch a pterodactyl for lunch. Wild Willie, the missing link, encounters a monster. 'The dinosaur is some battler and Wild Willie meets his Waterloo and is sent on his way to baboon heaven.' Ivoryhead chances upon the body and claims it as his own, planting his foot upon the baboon's chest in a gesture of triumph that would become an O'Brien trademark. In this little puppet comedy can be found elements that O'Brien and his disciples would use through half a century of spectacular cinema. Two years later he made a slightly more serious single-reel dinosaur fantasy, *The Ghost of*

Slumber Mountain (1919). This caught the interest of the other missing link in the *Lost World* story, Watterson R. Rothacker.

Rothacker, West Coast manager of Billboard, saw the potential in films for publicity as early as 1911. Forming the Industrial Motion Picture Company he evolved many specialized techniques: he used animation to make movies of Gus Edson's newspaper comic strip, *Old Doc Yak*. O'Brien joined Rothacker and together they created the monsters of *The Lost World*. Although their flickery dinosaur was outclassed by the dragon Fritz Lang built in Germany for *Siegfried* (1924), the American epic had the showman's touch. The erupting volcanoes, stampeding monsters, and destruction of London thrilled a vast audience who would have been bored by the turgid Teuton legend. The film still thrills as Professor Challenger lowers his binoculars and mouths the immortal subtitle, 'This is the greatest moment of my life. I have seen a living pterodactyl!'

Roland West, who had directed Lon Chaney in *The*

Cats and Canaries: Forrest Stanley and Laura La Plante were *The Cat and the Canary* (Universal 1927; *above*), silent style. *Opposite:* Paulette Goddard and friend in the Paramount sound remake (1939).

his old country, of course, and among his many imports for Universal was Paul Leni. Handed the script of John Willard's Broadway success of 1922, Leni turned *The Cat and the Canary* (1927) into something more than the now standard comedy-thriller. The plot remained preposterous: one of the surviving relatives of an eccentric millionaire dons monstrous makeup to scare the heiress out of her pretty mind. But the trappings were superb: cobwebs, clocks, corridors down which camera and characters raced with uncanny speed, curtains billowing like spectral shrouds. Even the opening titles frightened, and the first shot symbolized shudders to come: the dying man, dwarfed by gigantic bottles and snarling cats, dissolves into his spiky old castle.

Leni's first sight of the crouching monster is, like Julian's Phantom, a double thrill. The Cat emerges from a shadowed panel in the background and slowly creeps towards unsuspecting Laura La Plante. He pops behind the door, then his claw comes clutching round, groping for her throat like a giant spider. When she finally sees his hideous face – the Cat bobs round and comes up at her – Leni cuts to a quick closeup, rushing his lens into Laura's face as she screams. Cut to an animated subtitle in towering, shivering letters: 'HELP!' As

a sly nod to his old school, Leni had his sinister little doctor made up to recall Caligari. Small wonder the New York Times called it 'the first time that a mystery melodrama has been lifted into the realms of art'. Smaller wonder that other studios rushed aboard the bandwagon.

The Gorilla (1927), like Ralph Spence's play, built up the comedy relief: Keystone comic Charlie Murray played the lead. His inept detection brought shrieks of both kinds when he confronted the killer, an eight-foot ape. It was really Walter Pidgeon all the time. More of a thriller was the gorilla in *The Wizard* (1927). This 'fiend-faced ape' was played by George Kotsonaros, the 'Monk' who had lost out to Rin Tin Tin. An updated, dressed-up version of *Balaoo*, Gustav von Seyffertitz was mad Professor Paul Coriolos, commanding his creature to kidnap a judge's daughter in revenge for sentencing his son. MGM's *The Thirteenth Hour* (1927) had Lionel Barrymore as Professor Leroy, whose houseful of sliding panels and sinister sofas was operated from a secret switchboard. At 1 a.m. he would go out on murderous prowl, returning home in time to don a wig and a benign expression.

Benjamin Christensen was one more Continental import whose creativity suffered in the cause of commercialism. This Dane had directed an imaginative documentary called *Witchcraft Through the Ages* (1921). He himself played naked Satan, presiding over a Black Mass depicted in a detail unsurpassed by the permissive cinemas of half a century on. Naturally, First National gave him their *Cat and the Canary* cash-in to do. *The Haunted House* (1928), from the Owen Davis play of scared heirs and hidden bonds, complete with mad doctor, weird caretaker, and sexy somnambulist, was so successful that the team of Christensen, scenarist Richard Bee, and title-writer William Irish, were told to do it all again. *Seven Footprints to Satan* (1929), Abraham Merritt's classic fantasy of Devil worship, was even given the same twist ending: all was eventually exposed as actors hired to hoax.

It was the last silent scream of the horror film. The voice of Jolson the Jazz Singer was heard in the land and to some the sound of horror had already begun. It was the end of an art form. To a world full of Chaney fans there was but one question. Would the Man of a Thousand Faces become the Man of a Thousand Voices?

Made-over Monsters: Horror movies are the hardy perennials of the cinema: when the originals are too old to revive, new versions are made, such as Hammer's *The Phantom of the Opera* (1962; *left*) and Fox's *The Gorilla* (1939).

THRILLS ✚ LAUGHS ═ ENTERTAINMENT

THE *The* **RITZ BROTHERS**

in

GORILLA

ANITA LOUISE · PATSY KELLY · LIONEL ATWILL · BELA LUGOSI
JOSEPH CALLEIA · EDWARD NORRIS · WALLY VERNON

Directed by Allan Dwan · Associate Producer Harry Joe Brown · Screen play by Rian James
& Sid Silvers · Based on the Play by Ralph Spence · A 20th Century-Fox Picture ·

DARRYL F. ZANUCK *in Charge of Production*
LONDON TRADE SHOWS:

CENTURY THEATRE, SOHO SQUARE, W.1, **TO-DAY, JUNE 15th, 11** a.m. • **3** p.m. • **6.30** p.m.

Blood Suckers: Vampire variation on the romantic necking scene. Bela Lugosi bares Helen Chandler's jugular in *Dracula* (Universal 1931; *above left*) and Christopher Lee seeks Veronica Carlson's in *Dracula Has Risen From the Grave* (Hammer 1968; *left*). John Beal prepares to bite Colleen Grey in *The Vampire* (UA 1957; *above*), while a Philippino vampire takes a bloodthirsty bite in *The Blood Drinkers* (Hemisphere 1966; *opposite*).

Edward Van Sloan. Jack Pierce created the make-up, and with Karl Freund at the camera it may come as no surprise that the Monster looked like the Golem. Lugosi wore a broad wig and had a polished, clay-like skin. Said Van Sloan, 'He looked like something out of *Babes in Toyland!*'

Lugosi rejected the role, Laemmle rejected the tests, Florey rejected the film. Actor and director began work on adapting Poe and the project was shelved. Meanwhile James Whale, an English stage producer, had exceeded Laemmle's expectations with the romantic *Waterloo Bridge* (1931). Offered his pick of thirty properties, Whale chose *Frankenstein*: 'I thought it would be amusing to try and make what everybody knows is a physical impossibility seem believable.' Whale rejected Leslie Howard, Universal's choice for the title role. He wanted Colin Clive, the friend who had given so tense a reading of Captain Stanhope in Whale's stage and screen versions of *Journey's End* (1930). But who to cast as the Monster?

Lunching daily in the studio commissary, Whale's eyes searched among the crowds of eating actors. One face stood out, lean and hungry even after meals: a character player from the *Graft* set. Whale, once a cartoonist, began to sketch that haunting, heavy head.

'Boris Karloff's face fascinated me. I made drawings of his head, added sharp bony ridges where I imagined the skull might have joined. His physique was weaker than I could wish, but that queer, penetrating personality of his, I felt, was more important than his shape, which could easily be altered.'

It was not that easy, particularly for Karloff. For a fortnight he sat still in the makeup chair, a guinea-pig for Jack P. Pierce. The derivative Golem concept was thrown out in favour of scientific plausibility. Said Pierce:

'I did some research in anatomy, surgery, criminology, ancient and modern burial customs, and electrodynamics. I discovered there are six ways a surgeon can cut the skull, and I figured Dr Frankenstein, who was not a practising surgeon, would take the easiest. That is, he would cut the top of the skull off, straight across like a pot lid, hinge it, pop the brain in, and clamp it tight. That's the reason I decided to make the Monster's head square and flat like a box, and dig that big scar across his forehead, and have metal clamps hold it together. The two metal studs that stick out the sides of his neck are inlets for electricity – plugs. The Monster is an electrical gadget and lightning is his life force.'

Pierce built Karloff an overhanging brow with layers of cotton and rubber. He coated his eyelids with wax and pulled his mouth out and down with invisible wire clamps. Combinations of greasepaint were applied until he found a blue-green blend that photographed grey as a corpse. The dead ends of the fingers were easiest: Pierce simply blackened them with boot polish. Then came the costume:

'I made his arms look longer by shortening the sleeves of his coat. His legs were stiffened by steel struts and two pairs of pants. His large feet were the boots asphalt-spreaders wear.'

The complete kit, including a steel spine, weighed forty-eight pounds. The makeup took three-and-a-half hours to put on in the morning, an hour-and-a-half to remove at night. Karloff was led to and from the set, his head under a cloth; he ate alone. The film was shot entirely in an enclosed studio, under lights, in the heat of summer. Said Laemmle,

Club Member: John Barrymore was hypnotic as *The Mad Genius* (Warner 1931; *above*).
Laughing Boy: *Son of Kong* (RKO 1933).

'Karloff's eyes mirrored the suffering we needed.'

Frankenstein (1931) took up where *Dracula* left off, and not just with confidence in its horrors. The first film ended with Edward Van Sloan stepping out of character and screen to deliver a sinister epilogue on the vampire: 'There are such things.' As the second film began he was back with a prologue.

'How do you do. Mr Carl Laemmle feels it would be a little unkind to present this picture without just a word of friendly warning. We are about to unfold the story of Frankenstein, a man of science, who sought to create a man after his own image without reckoning upon God. It is one of the strangest tales ever told. It deals with the two great mysteries of creation, life and death. I think it will thrill you. It may even shock you. It might even horrify you. So if any of you do not care to subject your nerves to such a strain, now's your chance to. . . . Well, we've warned you!'

Despite Mr Carl's friendly warning, an hysterical Christmas preview at Santa Barbara produced so many threatening letters that the studio considerably revised the film before release. They shortened a scene by a river where the Monster floats flowers with his first friend, a little girl, then tries to float her; he is saddened when she sinks. The abrupt cut made things worse, adding awful implication when the child next appears, dead and draggled in the arms of her father. (English censors let the scene stand, preferring to shorten the sequence where the Monster invades Mae Clarke's bedroom. The implication, again, was worse than the intention.) A new ending was added showing Frankenstein recovering from his fatal fall while his jovial father toasted, 'Here's to a son of the house of Frankenstein': a prophetic phrase foretelling two sequels unborn.

James Whale gave Karloff the greatest entrance an actor could hope for. From the grave-robbing prologue, all is literally build-up until the man-made man lies, bandaged and shrouded, waiting for life. Fervid Frankenstein, student of chemical galvanism and electro-biology, has stitched together a body from pieces hacked from coffin and gibbet. In its skull lies a brain stolen from medical university by his hunchbacked assistant. Little does Henry know that Fritz dropped the chosen brain and brought an abnormal one instead.

Roast Ghosties: Boris Karloff and Catherine Lacey in *The Sorcerers* (Tigon 1967).

'Think of it, Fritz. The brain of a dead man waiting to live again – in a body I made with my own hands!' Henry has gone beyond the ultraviolet to discover 'the great ray that first brought life into the world'. At the height of a storm he raises his man through the roof of the tower laboratory, bathing him with lightning. The table is lowered; one hand raises slowly: 'It's alive! It's alive!' Fadeout.

Audience tension, stretched to a peak, is stretched even further as Whale makes us wait through some 'light relief' for our first sight of the Monster. At last it comes. The set is darkened, silent save for the sound of heavy footfalls. A door opens and the Monster looms out of the darkness – backwards! Whale cuts in for a closeup of the back of his head. The Monster turns slowly, moving his face into the light. Then Whales cuts and cuts again, each time closer in on that awful face. Back he goes to long-shot as the new-born man ('He's only a few days old') leans alarmingly towards his maker. Frankenstein's beckoning gestures, the Monster's lurching steps, recall Wegener and his Golem. But totally new, touchingly pathetic, are Karloff's hand movements as the scientist opens a trap in the roof to let his creation see daylight for the first time. Like the baby that he is, the Monster reaches out to grasp the sun. His cold grey body finds more than warmth in the fiery torch the hunchback uses to tame and torture him. The Monster has all our sympathy when, at the end, he hurls the creator who rejected him at the howling mob and dies, shrieking, pinned beneath a beam in a burning windmill.

Once in Karloff's long, lean years, he had hitched a lift from Lon Chaney. The star, no stranger to the hard grind of bit-part work, told Karloff his secret. 'Find something no one else can do and they'll begin to take notice of you.' Said Karloff, 'When I was offered the part of the Monster I knew that I'd found it at last. The part was what we call a "natural". Any actor who played it was destined for success.' Modest Boris, for not one of the actors who followed in his eighteen-pound boots achieved his stature.

Carl Laemmle had found his new Lon Chaney.

The Universal Monsters scared more than the audience and the censors: the other studios were frightened they might lose some of the action. Paramount got in first, timing *Murder by the Clock* (1931) to beat Frankenstein into the cinemas. Irving Pichel gibbered, and graveyards yawned: so did the audience. 'The blood-chilling mystery of a man who was murdered twice' lacked that new

Classic Karloff: *Frankenstein* (Universal 1931) was billed as 'The Man Who Made a Monster'; it was the film that made a star. Boris Karloff, a long-standing small-part player, stomped to stardom as the synthetic yet soulful creation of Colin Clive (*opposite above*), unnatural victim of nature's freak, Dwight Frye (*opposite below left*). Karloff's creature was unique: often copied, never equalled. Christopher Lee in *The Curse of Frankenstein* (Hammer 1957; *opposite below right*) was forced to use new makeup (by Phil Leakey) as Jack P. Pierce's format was copyrighted by Universal.

touch of the supernatural that distinguished the true horror film. Pichel would find slightly steadier work as a director, but meanwhile his curious looks made him a convenient Karloff substitute. Paramount were pleased enough to revive for him their old success, *Dr Jekyll and Mr Hyde* (1931), but the poor man was instantly rejected by the director. Said Rouben Mamoulian, 'I wanted someone who could play Jekyll and Pichel could only play Hyde!' Mamoulian asked for Fredric March, a light comedian who was a ringer for the young Barrymore. Paramount objected; Mamoulian insisted; March won the Academy Award – the only Monster with an Oscar.

'For six weeks I had to arrive at the studios each morning at 6 a.m., so that Wally Westmore could spend four hours building pieces on my nose and cheeks, sticking fangs in my mouth, and pushing cotton wool up my nostrils.'

Rouben Mamoulian, Russian-born man of the theatre, was obsessed by that legendary full-view transformation by Richard Mansfield. He determined to devise a one-take change for his star. March was coated with successive layers of make-up, each more detailed than the last, each in a different colour. By holding colour transparencies in front of the camera and removing them one by one, the change from Jekyll to Hyde filtered through on to the film.

Mamoulian used the 'moving camera' subjectively to draw his audience into the picture and the very mind of his monster. In the beginning we are Jekyll, moving through his doctor's day, seeing our face only in his mirror. Later, as he raises the fatal phial to his lips, we again click into his eyes. The laboratory spins about us (Karl Struss tied to the top of his camera was revolved to secure this 360-degree pan); our blood pounds in our ears (Mamoulian ran up and down stairs recording his own heartbeats); until again we see our face, our new face, in the mirror. It is a moment of revenge for every movie monster: we who came to stare see only ourselves.

'Grimmer than *Dracula*, More Gruesome than *Frankenstein*!' Yardsticks already, the originals were used by Universal to boost their third entry, *Murders in the Rue Morgue* (1932). Lugosi, in fetching curls and overgrown eyebrows, was more evil than ever in costume (*Dracula* lost much of its mood by being set in the present), and Robert Florey emerged at last as a director of power. However, that Frenchman's conception of 1845 Paris was more like Gothic Holstenwall. Even Poe's plot came out like Dr Caligari, as Dr Mirakle, a sideshow hypnotist, commands Erik the gorilla to abduct frail Camille over the rooftops of Paris. Hunched Janos the Black One (Noble Johnson) aids Mirakle in his sadistic experiments, which involve strung-up prostitutes and transfusions of gorilla blood. The pioneer of demonic Darwinism is climactically strangled by his revolting pet.

The Hollywood pattern was ever one of cycles, and Universal had clearly started a new one. The British Board of Film Censors did not like it to start with and now that a new element, sex, was creeping in they liked it even less. The Soho erotics of Mamoulian's Mr Hyde were so explicit that in the British release print, Miriam Hopkins hardly appeared. But it was not sex that was the trouble with Tod Browning's latest picture. *Freaks* (1932) was banned outright in Britain. It even upset MGM, who produced it: after a spotty, press-protesting release they 'lost' it in their vaults. *Freaks* remains unique, the ultimate extension of the Quasimodo syndrome, the fascination of deformity taken to the *n*th degree – because there are such things.

Browning was back in his beloved world of sideshows and suckers. Upon the short story 'Spurs' by Clarence 'Tod' Robbins (he of *The Unholy Three*) Browning created a carnival of horrors. Harry Earles (again from *The Three*) is the midget who inherits a fortune. This makes him instantly

MURDERS IN THE RUE MORGUE

CARL LAEMMLE PRESENTS

EDGAR ALLAN POE'S
DRAMATIC STORY OF
THE HORRORS OF PARIS

Grimmer than that grim picture, "DRACULA," more gruesome and awe-inspiring than "FRANKENSTEIN," EDGAR ALLAN POE'S remarkable mystery story "MURDERS IN THE RUE MORGUE," laid in the dark caverns of Paris, will thrill you to your finger-tips. Beautifully enacted by

BELA LUGOSI and **SIDNEY FOX**
The Original "DRACULA" · Star of "STRICTLY DISHONORABLE"
Directed by ROBERT FLOREY

Murders and Monkeys: Irving Pichel was Paramount's answer to Karloff in *Murder by the Clock* (1931; *opposite*). Universal already had their answer in Bela Lugosi. He objected to the Monster makeup, but not to the curls and eyebrows of *Murders in the Rue Morgue* (1931; *below*). Warner remade it in 3D as *Phantom of the Rue Morgue* (1954; *bottom*).

his fierce face and sly eyeballs bridged a curious gap between Mittel-European police inspectors and mad doctors. Atwill continued a tradition that had begun with Karloff: in Hollywood horror, British was best. Karloff, Clive, Atwill; shortly Banks and Rains and Rathbone; then Hardwicke and Zucco and even Skelton Knaggs. Was there something especially sinister built into the British accent – it even echoes in the speech of Vincent Price from Missouri – or was it that to German-born movie-makers English was 'foreign'?

The one great exception was Bela Lugosi. His chill lilt thrilled, but audiences found there was too much mystery in his movies: they couldn't understand what he was talking about. His early refusal to learn English, other than phonetically, was finally catching up with him. Only two major horror movies behind him and already he was working for the Halperin Brothers in their independent (i.e. cut-price) production, *White Zombie* (1932). This pictorial story of mesmerism and the walking dead was beautifully photographed (Arthur Martinelli), hauntingly scored (a Negro spiritual called 'Listen to the Lambs'), and atrociously acted. It was as moody a piece of visual mystery as the old days of silence ever wrought. Lugosi, talented when type-cast, played Legendre, a man known as Murder. Zombie-master to the trade, he supplied cut-price labour for the local sugar mills: corpses resurrected from recent graves and animated by his power of mind over matter. He went nowhere without his bodyguard, a crew for whom motley was hardly the word. 'Who are they?' shrilled the hero, and Lugosi replied, 'For you, my friend, they are the Angels of Death.'

After being thwarted in his plot to zombify Madge Bellamy, poisoned on her wedding day and held in his mountain eyrie, the Land of the Living Dead, Legendre and his eerie entourage go over the ramparts to end on the rocks. But while Lugosi was feeling the first chilly wind of change that blew less from the mountains of Transylvania than the Hills of Beverly, Karloff went from strength to strength. As the mute brute Morgan it took Melvyn Douglas, Raymond Massey and Charles Laughton to hold him down.

The Old Dark House (1932) was the full British horror bit, set in Universal's Wales. James Whale directed Yorkshire Laughton's Hollywood debut. The group that is forced to spend a stormbound night in the Femm family home is less ill-assorted than that family itself. Scion is Horace, played by Ernest Thesiger at his most nostrilled. A fugitive, he is a more feminine Femm than his sister, deaf and dirty Rebecca (Eva Moore), who cries 'No beds! They can't have beds!' as she serves up the black-eyed potatoes. Upstairs is the bedridden head of the family, Sir Roderick, age 102. His youthful excesses are responsible for the wrath now closing in, according to religious Rebecca. The old wretch was played by Elspeth Dudgeon under the more suitable pseudonym, John. Up another flight, behind a padlocked door, is yet a further Femm: Saul, 'the cleverest of us all'.

Morgan the mighty butler hits the bottle and unlocks Saul. A small white hand hovers on the banister. . . . The worst horror of them all turns out to be a little fellow, an old child, pathetic in his pleadings for freedom. Saul wins everybody's sympathy, but when nobody but us is looking his face slips into a snarl. Saul has a secret: he has discovered flame does not burn. It is cold, like ice, and cuts like a knife. He proves it by setting the house on fire.

Whale took his tale from J.B.Priestley's 1927 novel 'Benighted', bringing in Balderston, Benn Levy, and his old friend R.C.Sherriff from *Journey's End* to script. These literary intellects suited Whale, who liked to lighten his frights with twists of wit. Where his grotesque taste had leavened *Frankenstein* with the muttering scuttlings of Dwight Frye, hobbling along on a foot-high walking-stick, *The Old Dark House* was thick with eccentrics.

Karloff, scraggle-jowled and scarred, on no more dialogue than 'Grunt', again stirred a strange sympathy. He clasps his dead friend Saul to his chest, whimpering and rocking him like some awful baby. Karloff spoke for the first time in his second career in *The Mask of Fu Manchu* (1932). He played the devil doctor on loan-out to MGM, accentuating his natural lisp to achieve the snake-like hissing as prescribed by Sax Rohmer. In his mad bid to conquer the world for the yellow races, Fu used fiendish tortures lit with all MGM's gloss.

Camerawork was also a cornerstone of Karloff's Christmas box: Laemmle promoted Karl Freund. That photographer's debut as director was *The Mummy* (1932). Balderston opened his screenplay with a subtitle:

'This is the Scroll of Thoth. Herein are set down the magic words by which Isis raised Osiris from the dead. Oh! Amon-Ra. Oh! God of Gods. Death is but the doorway to new life. . . . We live today.

Beauties and Beasts: Fredric March and Miriam Hopkins in *Dr Jekyll and Mr Hyde* (Paramount 1931); Boris Karloff and Gloria Stuart in *The Old Dark House* (Universal 1932).

'. . . We shall live again. In many forms shall we return, Oh Mighty One.'

As Bramwell Fletcher murmurs these words, the long-dead eyelids of an ancient mummy quiver open to reveal a Golem-like gleam of life. A breath, then silently the revived corpse crosses the room, takes the Scroll, and slips into the Egyptian night, trailing tatty bandages and leaving young Fletcher a laughing madman: 'He went for a little walk!' Ten years later, a dry old man called Ardath Bey helps David Manners uncover the lost tomb of Princess Anck-es-en-Amon. Bey and the mummy are the same man: Im-Ho-Tep, High Priest of the Temple of the Sun at Karnak, buried alive 3,700 years ago for daring to try to revive the dead Princess. 'Sentenced to death not only in this world, but the next.'

Zita Johann as the daughter of the Governor of Sudan becomes strangely possessed, speaking 'words not heard on this Earth for two thousand years'. The Mummy intends eternal reunion with his reincarnated princess, which can be achieved only by her death. Breaking free of his mesmeric thrall, she calls upon Isis for help. The statue of the Goddess comes to life and mystically reduces Im-Ho-Tep to ancient dust.

The Mummy consolidated Karloff as a character star in the Chaney mould. Ironically, the crumbling creature was created out of 'beauty clay', applied between layers of cotton by Jack P. Pierce. Once bandaged and caked, Karloff could scarcely move, and the effort to speak through the cracking clay helped him to create the grate of a 3,700-year-old throat. He was billed by surname alone, 'Karloff the Uncanny', a cinematic accolade hitherto confined to Garbo.

Lugosi, who had lost his chance of the Chaney crown, was now forced to take the makeup chair. As the Sayer of the Law in *The Island of Lost Souls* (1932), Lugosi said the Law: 'Not to spill blood. That is the Law. Are we not men?' He said it through a faceful of fur, for the Sayer was a humanized animal. The Law was that of Dr Moreau, Charles Laughton at his sweaty best. This sadistic vivisectionist rules his private Pacific isle with whip and knife. In his House of Pain he has bypassed a thousand years of evolution. His creations include faithful M'Ling (Tetsu Komai), a former dog; snouty Gola (Harry Ezekian), ex-pig; apish Ouran (Hans Steinke), once a monkey. His big success is Lota the Panther Woman, played by Kathleen Burke (winner of the Panther Woman of America contest). Lota's Achilles heel is her fingernails: they extrude under stress – 'The stub-born beast-flesh creeping back.' This gives the game away when Moreau seeks to mate her with shipwrecked Richard Arlen. At the end the revolting creatures take their creator to his House of Pain. Like *Freaks*, but unlike Tod Browning, Erle C. Kenton leaves the screaming end-product to our imagination. Also like *Freaks*, the film was banned outright by the British censor, much to the delight of H.G.Wells (from whose novel 'The Island of Dr Moreau' it was adapted) and the fury of film fans.

Fay Wray's scream when used as bait to catch the Moon Monster of *Dr X*, made her the First Lady of the Horror Film. Born in Alberta in 1907, a grounding in Hal Roach comedies seemed unlikely training for her new career. She was teamed again twice with Lionel Atwill, first in *The Vampire Bat* (1933). Atwill played Dr Otto Von Niemann of Kleinschloss, who hypnotized his butler to supply fresh victims for his unconventional research. The vampire killings were cover-ups for something more horrid, and only Melvyn Douglas as Inspector Karl Breetschneider was able to save Fay Wray from a transfusion of Atwill's 'blood substitute'.

The Mystery of the Wax Museum (1933) saw Atwill and Fay Wray teamed in two-colour Technicolor. It brought the old Chaney style back to cinema, the horror of disfigurement. Atwill was Ivan Igor, waxworks sculptor, who lost both income and reason when his partner burned their museum for the insurance. The melting of the wax figures is an early touch of nastiness. Escaping the holocaust, seemingly unsinged but confined to a wheelchair, Igor sets up again. This time he snatches bodies and even murders to obtain models for his exhibition, coating the corpses with wax. Fay Wray exposes the mystery and Atwill, too, for as her fists flail at his face his whole head cracks away to reveal the burned, scarred and two-colour Technicolored mess beneath. The first great unmasking in modern horror movies, it remains a moment unequalled in the memories of millions, including Miss Wray.

> 'I was in his clutches and I had to hit him in the face. It was necessary for the audience to see this and be shocked. But when I struck him, and the moment I saw part of him, I just froze! I wanted to run; I just couldn't go on! So they had to make another mask and do it over when I recovered.'

But for Fay Wray the horror was only beginning. There were bigger things in store.

Monster's Mummy: Boris Karloff as *The Mummy* (Universal 1932).

THE KING OF KONGS

In which King Kong has a Son, Frankenstein has a Bride, Dracula has a Daughter, and the Devil has a Doll.

Fay Wray was at RKO-Radio as the title role in *The Most Dangerous Game* (1932): pursued through a foggy, boggy jungle by a Russian Count with a Tartar bow and *The Hounds of Zaroff* – which was the British title for this exciting expansion of Richard Connell's award-winning short story. Leslie Banks played the twisted sadistic aristocrat, a Hollywood debut for the British actor continuing the sinister tradition. Zaroff gave his pretty prey a head start in more ways than one. His trophy room was hung with stuffed souvenirs of similar hunts. This scene was too much for Britain: the censor, Zaroff-like, chopped it off. Fay Wray learned it had all been a dummy run when she was summoned by the producer.

'Mr Cooper said to me that he had an idea for a film in mind. The only thing he'd tell me was that I was going to have the tallest, darkest leading man in Hollywood. Naturally, I thought of Clark Gable.' What she got was King Kong.

Merian Coldwell Cooper, a Florida-born flier, soldier of fortune and journalist, had joined forces with an ex-Keystone Comedy cameraman named Ernest B. Schoedsack to create the American documentary. Their *Grass* (1925) and *Chang* (1927) are classics of authentic adventure – yet it is through their fantastic fiction of *King Kong* (1933) that they will be ever remembered in cinema history.

'Out of an uncharted, forgotten corner of the world, a monster . . . surviving seven million years of evolution . . . crashes into the haunts of civilization . . . on to the talking screen . . . to stagger the imagination of man!'

Those words in the Souvenir Programme hardly prepared audiences for the film that was about to unreel. 'The Strangest Story Ever Conceived by Man!' . . . 'The Greatest Film the World Will Ever See!' For once the catchlines were right. In the history of horror movies, indeed of movies, *King Kong* still towers above them all.

Kong, the fifty-foot King of Skull Island, somewhere south-west of Sumatra, had in reality a bigger build-up than even the fifty mist-wreathed minutes that precede the shock of his first in-film appearance. The movie was three years in the making, more if you include a pilot piece of prehistoric monster animation made for Harry O. Hoyt's abandoned project, *Creation*. This model work had been done by Willis O'Brien, man of *The Lost World*, and it caught the eye of David O. Selznick, newly arrived at RKO as vice-president in charge of production. He showed the reel to Merian C. Cooper, who had already come up with an idea about an outsize ape. Instead of expensive location shooting, could Cooper construct his giant gorilla idea entirely in the studio, using animation?

Edgar Wallace, whose play 'The Terror' had been the first horror Talkie, arrived from London on 5 December 1931. He had an eight-week contract with RKO to script a horror film. Three days later he wrote to his wife, 'I am also doing a story of prehistoric life!' For inspiration they ran him *Dracula* ('Crude horror stuff, but I must say it raised my hair a little bit') and *Murder by the Clock* ('The actor was the very man I want for my horror story'*), and on the 12th Cooper took him to see O'Brien making another test, a process shot.

'The camera shoots against a blue background lit up by about fifty orange arc lamps. It was two men making an attack upon a prehistoric beast. The beast, of course, was not there: he is put in afterwards, and every movement of the men is controlled by a man who is seeing the beast through a moviola, and signals by means of a bell every movement that the men make.'

* Irving Pichel. He did not, in the end, act in it; he directed it! (*Before Dawn*, 1933.)

King of Swing: *King Kong Versus Godzilla* (Toho 1962).

This was the Dunning Process in action. On 30 December Wallace saw the finished scenes: 'They were not particularly good, though there was one excellent sequence where a man is chased by a dinosaurus.' Wallace went into the animation room, a projection room converted into a workshop. O'Brien had completed the skeleton and framework of 'the giant monkey which appears in this play' (the King was as yet unchristened).

'I saw a woodcarver fashioning the skull on which the actual figure will be built. In another place was a great scale model of a gigantic gorilla, which had been made specially. One of the gorilla figures will be nearly thirty feet high. All round the walls are wooden models of prehistoric beasts. There are two miniature sets with real miniature trees, on which the prehistoric animals are made to gambol. Only fifty feet can be taken a day of the animating part. Every move of the animal had to be fixed by the artist, including the ripples of his muscles. Of course it is a tedious job.'

To anyone but a man of Willis O'Brien's devotion. Kong and the other models had to be separately photographed every time their position was changed a sixteenth of an inch. Said O'Brien, 'We worked ten hours a day – the fight between Kong and the pterodactyl took seven weeks to film!'

O'Brien had his work on *The Lost World* to guide him, but this time there was a brand-new problem. Since 1925 the movies had learned to talk: what did a prehistoric monster *sound* like? Murray Spivak of RKO's sound department built forty noise-making instruments in all. To vocalize an arsinotherium he blew a column of air through a vox humana pipe from an old organ. He next re-recorded this hiss at a subnormal speed: lowering it an octave added a note of terror. Then he reversed the soundtrack and slowed that down yet another octave. For other monsters he recorded the growls of cougars, leopards and lions, reversing them to obtain previously unknown noises. His biggest problem, of course, was Kong. The type of sound made by a prehistoric ape would naturally relate to its present-day descendant, but a gorilla's growl was less than effective: Kong was fifty feet tall. Recording gorilla cries backwards at a slow speed was part of the answer, the rest was a specially built sound-box 25 feet square. This came in handy for hollow thumps when the great ape beat his chest.

Cooper had key scenes sketched in detail before the film went on the floor, and no fewer than twenty-seven models of Kong were made, in different sizes but all to scale with the ape's official vital statistics:

Height	50 ft
Face	7 ft from hairline to chin
Nose	2 ft
Lips	6 ft from corner to corner
Brows	4 ft 3 in
Mouth	6 ft when stretched as in a smile
Eyes	Each 10 in long
Ears	1 ft long
Eye-teeth	10 in high, 7 in at base
Molars	14 in round, 4 in high
Chest	60 ft in repose
Legs	15 ft
Arms	23 ft
Reach	75 ft

When Kong reached for Fay Wray and examined her curiously, peeling off what was left of her clothes, the half-minute scene took twenty-three hours to film.

'They had a huge rubber arm with a steel cable inside large enough to hold me. The fingers were pressed around my waist and then, by leverage, they lifted me up into the air. All the closeups were done that way. There was a tiny little doll model used for when King Kong was holding me. It was about three inches long. I couldn't tell the difference when I would go to see the day's work, it was blended that well.'

Kong's name came from Cooper's fondness for mysterious monosyllables. Selznick liked the title, but the New York office objected: they thought it too much like his *Chang* and *Rango*. They publicized it as *The Beast*. Wallace suggested *King Ape* in January 1931, and although the completed picture was actually advertised as simply *Kong* in January 1933, it was finally combined with Wallace's title for copyright registration on 24 February 1933 as *King Kong*: exactly one year after Wallace's death.

King Kong had a monster première: it opened at the world's two largest theatres, the Radio City Music Hall and the Roxy in New York, simul-

Losing Face: ''E's all eaten away!' screams Una O'Connor of Claude Rains, *The Invisible Man* (Universal 1933; *above*). Ilona Massey was touched by Jon Hall, *The Invisible Agent* (Universal 1942; *below*).

Monster's Mate: James Whale made the best modern horror movie, or the worst, according to your taste. Whale's taste was for the bizarre and in *Bride of Frankenstein* (Universal 1935) it ran as amok as his Monster. Whale mocked the crucifixion (*opposite above*) and the marriage ceremony (*below*) as well as the Hollywood Romantic Co-star Poster. He even overturned religious symbols (*left*). The Monster was Karloff, of course, and his Mate was Elsa Lanchester. A typical Whale twist was to cast her as the story's authoress Mary Wollstonecraft Shelley, as well: creator and created.

taneously: the only picture ever to do so. Ten thousand seats packed for ten shows a day: for escapist entertainment there was clearly no Depression. *King Kong* came in at 650,000 dollars: it is still making money. When unloosed on television for the first time, one New York station ran it sixteen times in seven days.

Film producer-cum-explorer Robert Armstrong charters *The Venture* and steams off for Skull Island, armed with a map, a camera, and Fay Wray. The natives are unfriendly until they see her. Soon Fay finds herself chained to two pillars while a witch-doctor, accompanied by Max Steiner's magnificent music, chants: 'Wa Saba ani mako, O Tar Vey, Rama Kong' . . . 'Thy bride is here, O mighty one, great Kong!' Crashing down the overgrown undergrowth comes her hairy husband, to bear Fay away to his primordial lair. Bruce Cabot braves many a monster before gassing the groom with grenades. The unconscious Kong is shipped to America and exhibited as the Eighth Wonder of the World.

'He was a King and a God in the world he knew, but now he comes to civilization merely a captive, a show to gratify your curiosity.' Dazzled by a thousand flashbulbs, Kong breaks his chains and rampages through New York. He finds his bride again and climbs to the top of the Empire State Building. Army planes swoop at him like mosquitoes; their machine-guns more than sting. Gently, the weakening King sets down his little Queen and falls, one hundred and two storeys, to his death. His captor speaks his epitaph: 'It was beauty killed the beast.'

The incredible success called for a sequel and Cooper and Schoedsack rushed *Son of Kong* (1933) into the cinemas for Christmas. Shorter by thirty minutes than the original's one hundred, the replay gave full rein to O'Brien's humour. Where he had given the father moments of charming humanity, he made the son such a clown that the film had to be subtitled 'A Serio-Comic Phantasy'.

Robert Armstrong, dunned for the damages caused by his discovery, flees to the South Seas in the good old *Venture*. His plan, to pay his debts with Kong's long-lost treasures. This time Helen Mack is the dark-eyed lovely taken along for the ride. Kong Junior, a white-haired ape, becomes attached to the explorers, following them around like a faithful dog, boxing a bear and otherwise coming in handy when prehistoric monsters threaten. The climatic earthquake is spectacular and touching: young Kong gives his life to hold the humans above the tidal wave.

Both Kongs were scripted by Ruth Rose (Mrs Merian C. Cooper) and directed by the ex-cameraman Ernest B. Schoedsack, but only the funny son was considered horrific enough to notify the Home Office. This was the current treatment given to the horror film by the British Board of Film Censors when they felt their 'A' for Adults Only certificate was insufficient warning. One other Kong spin-off upset them, too: *King Klunk* (1933) makes its niche in history by being the first cartoon film branded 'Horrific'. It starred Pooch the Pup.

With animated horror the latest craze, who in Hollywood needed the original stars? Neither Karloff nor Lugosi wanted to know about Laemmle's latest project, conceived as yet another field day for the Special Effects department. The star was to remain unseen until the final frame.

The Invisible Man (1933) again demonstrated the horror film's potential for creating new stars. Overnight Claude Rains, who had been knocking around in British films since the early twenties, became a world star: the little man who wasn't there. He played the entire movie swathed in bandages and black goggles. Only his voice, that soft-spoken English so essential to the genre, carried the thriller through to the final, death-bed materialization. He was helped by his dialogue, brilliantly adapted from H.G.Wells' 1897 novel by R.C.Sherriff. As he elaborates upon his projected reign of terror, the Invisible One (as he was billed) laughs: 'Even the moon is frightened of me, frightened to death! The whole world is frightened to death!'

James Whale directed, and peopled his snow-bound village of Iping with the expected grotesques. Una O'Connor screamed at the drop of a tray as Mrs Jenny Hall, landlady of the Lion's Head, and E.E.Clive drooped a solemn walrus as P.C. Jaffers. When their strange visitor unpeels his bandaged face to reveal – nothing – stalwart Jaffers keeps his head. "E's invisible, that's wot's the matter with 'im!' Only Whale would dare show his monster as a pair of disembodied trousers, skipping down the lane singing 'Here we come gathering nuts in May!' Or a farmer reporting the discovery of the transparent fugitive with an awed, 'There's breathin' in me barn!' Whale was the only director in the golden age of horror to realize the danger of the unwanted laugh. He gave his nervous audience relief from tension by letting them laugh with, instead of at, the film.

Jack Griffin was a dedicated research scientist. He had been experimenting with monocaine, a

Locked in the Laboratory: No horror movie can be considered complete without a lab scene, and here is a selection of Universal's finest. Henry Frankenstein's original was enlarged and augmented for *Bride of Frankenstein* (1935; *left*), demolished and renovated for *Frankenstein Meets the Wolf Man* (1942; *top right*). Claude Rains' portable lab in *The Invisible Man* (1933; *top left*) was a do-it-yourself variation on Henry Hull's equipment for *Werewolf of London* (1935; *above*).

Battle Royal: King Kong squares up usually to Queensberry rules: Willis O'Brien, his animator, was a fight fan. Fay Wray is at the ringside in *King Kong* (RKO 1933; *right*), Robert Armstrong and Helen Mack in *Son of Kong* (RKO 1933; *opposite left*), but only the audience watches *King Kong Escapes* (Toho 1967; *opposite right*). One of the King's ringers was *Konga* (Cohen 1961; *below*).

EDGAR WALLACE'S Last Story

KING KONG

The Strangest Story ever conceived by man

COLISEUM
CHARING CROSS

Daily from noon
Sundays 6 £ 8·30 p·m·

Prices 1/3 - 8/6

drug from India. Tried on the dog it bleached the beast white and sent it raving mad. Griffin injected himself and became invisible. He went into hiding to work on an antidote, but, 'the drug seemed to light up my brain. Suddenly I realized the power I held, the power to rule, to make the world grovel at my feet.' He embarks on his Reign of Terror: murdering, robbing, derailing trains. But invisibility has its problems, as he explains to his unwilling associate, Kemp.

'I must always remain in hiding for an hour after meals. The food is visible inside me until it is digested. I can only work on fine, clear days. If I work in the rain the water can be seen on my head and shoulders. In fog you can see me like a bubble. In smoky cities, the soot settles on me like a dark outline. You must always be at hand to wipe off my feet, Kemp – even dirt under my fingernails would give me away.'

In the end Nature, as ever, abhors a vacuum: her snow shows his naked footfalls. A police inspector shoots – and suddenly there is a long dent in the smooth snow.

John P. Fulton, Universal's special effects man spent six months working out the several kinds of camera tricks. Some were done with 'invisible' wires (as when Griffin takes a cigarette or suddenly rocks a chair), others depended on an old conjurer's gimmick: a man completely clad in black is invisible against a black background. Details of the picture were painted out of the negative by retouchers working through microscopes with minute brushes, and there was double, triple, and more exposure, of course. Some tricks were new, others went back

to the days of Georges Méliès, who had shown the way with *Siva the Invisible* in 1904. But whilst the whole hit a new high in an age of cinematic miracles, it was Rains' reading of the lines that made his the face the world most wanted to see. It was a triumph of man over machine. Besides, Rains gave horror-film heroes their most famous last words: 'I meddled in things that man must leave alone.'

The Hollywood family Laemmle, having fathered and grandfathered the horror film, could see their creation fading out under the weight of expensive special effects. They revived the corpse with a showmanlike shot in the arm: two monsters for the price of one.

'It's Tremonstrous!' screamed the posters: 'Frankenstein Karloff, plus Dracula Lugosi plus Edgar Allan Poe!' Poor Poe, billed last, came off worst. By the time the British censor got through with it, *The Black Cat* (1934) itself, a supernatural reincarnation of female into feline, was seen so briefly that the film had to be retitled *The House of Doom*. Edgar G. Ulmer, the director, had been a set designer for Reinhardt in the theatre and Murnau in the movies, and much of the curious look of *The Black Cat* was his doing. Instead of the traditional trappings of cobwebby castle, Ulmer created an incredible, futuristic fort. The striking sets and way-out wardrobe caught Karloff's interest, for he had determined to play no more monsters. Karloff was cast as avant-garde architect Hjalmar Poelzig, whilst Lugosi bore the equally unlikely name of Vitus Verdegast. The co-stars' roles were weighted with care, for the first time siding Lugosi with the angels. Karloff, indeed, conducted a cult of devil-

Vampire Variants: The vampire remains the most indestructible of all movie monsters – there are more vampire films than any other genre-within-the-genre. Funny vampires include an encounter between Bela Lugosi and Old Mother Riley on one hand, and Roman Polanski's black satire *Dance of the Vampires* (Filmways 1967) on the other. Boxer Terry Downes made a particularly unpleasant apparition in the latter (*right*). Richard Matheson's vampiric variation 'I Am Legend' has been filmed twice with varying success. Vincent Price played *The Last Man On Earth* (Regina 1964; *below right*) and Charlton Heston *The Omega Man* (Seltzer 1971; *below left*). Rosalind Cash as a bleached Negress was perhaps a more alluring menace than the traditional clutching hand.

VINCENT PRICE in
"THE LAST MAN ON EARTH"
cert X
RELEASED BY GOLDEN ERA FILM DISTRIBUTORS

worshippers in his private chapel: or so the cock-eyed crucifixes would hint. In England, the censor switched Satanism to sun-worship.

David Manners, as ever, is the honeymooning hero *en route* to Budapest when a train crash injures his bride. Lugosi takes them along to Karloff's place, where the girl soon finds herself earmarked for sacrifice at the next session. Lugosi, fifteen years a prisoner of war, is seeking vengeance on his betrayer. In the interim Karloff has done more: he married Lugosi's wife, keeps her corpse under glass, and made a mistress of her daughter. Initial courtesy is thrown overboard as climaxes pile up. Karloff pumps his organ at a Black Mass; Lugosi saves the bride from sacrifice; Karloff is skinned alive; Lugosi is shot by the uncomprehending hero; the honeymooners escape as the dying Lugosi blows the minefield beneath the bizarre building; The End.

As if to atone, Universal produced a picture on a horror theme that was so serious in its approach that the British censor banned it outright. Of all horror films, *Life Returns* (1934) is the most 'lost'. Never seen in England, even in today's relaxed climate; never reprinted for television; unpreserved by archives, unmentioned by historians, unregistered even for copyright; yet it was the only 'documentary' horror film. It concluded with a sequence actually showing the dead restored to life. Dr Robert E. Cornish of the University of California revived a dead dog and filmed himself doing it. The rest of *Life Returns* was fiction, concocted by director Eugene Frenke with his writers James Hogan, John Goodrich, Arthur Homan, Wolfe Gilbert and Mary McCarthy.

Onslow Stevens, formerly the invisible scientist of Universal's science-fiction serial *The Vanishing Shadow* (1934), played John Kendrick, a doctor devoted to seeking a formula to restore life after death. He succeeds when his son's pet, called Lazarus of course, is gassed by the dog-catcher. The triumph also revives the boy's faith. Valerie Hobson played the doctor's wife: a dummy run for a bride to be.

'Alone you have created a man. Now, together, we will create his mate.'
'You mean . . . ?'
'Yes! A woman! That should be *really* interesting!'

The discussion between Dr Pretorius, eccentric experimenter, and Henry Frankenstein, reluctant collaborator, echoed an earlier discussion between two other, more real, monster-makers. Carl Laemmle Jr and James Whale were the Burke and Hare of the movie business. But these latter-day resurrectionists were not content with merely digging up the dead for money. They became the first men to bring the dead back to life (excluding, of course, Dr Robert E. Cornish).

'Who will be *The Bride of Frankenstein*? Who will dare?' The questions shouted by Universal Publicists were not answered by Whale's cast-list. It read 'The Monster's Mate . . . ????' A fuss had been made of testing both Phyllis Brooks and Brigitte Helm (the ex-robotrix of *Metropolis*) but in the end the part went to Elsa Lanchester. Or to Valerie Hobson, according to your interpretation of the title. The bride of Frankenstein was certainly Miss Hobson, while the mate of the Monster (Karloff) was undoubtedly Miss Lanchester. It is typical of Whale's turn of humour that he should see the part as a *doppelgänger*, both in title, and in concept: he had Elsa Lanchester play both the authoress, Mary Shelley, and her fictional creation. So pretty in the prologue, Miss Lanchester found herself built up on stilts from five-foot-four to a towering seven, and bound so tightly in bandages that she had to be carried about the studio and fed by tube. 'It was a horrible experience,' she said, 'It would have been easy to grow hysterical.'

The Bride's fantastic face was conceived by Whale and Ernest Thesiger, a refugee from *The Old Dark House*. Both men were artistic: Whale had cartooned for a London magazine and Thesiger was a crochet king. Using Queen Nefertiti as their inspiration, they designed 'a creature born of a thunderstorm, a wild jungle animal in captivity, with a suggestion of pride and dignity'. Their end-product, executed by Jack P. Pierce, enlivened by the Lanchester talent, made a memorable Mate.

Pierce had a busy time with two monsters to make up each day. Karloff alone took seven hours to construct, starting at 6 a.m. with the greasepaint, collodion and cotton, and ending at 1 p.m. with the steel braces, padded suit and boots. Then, at the end of a long day's shoot, would come the dismantling. He was lucky to be home by nine. There were modifications to makeup and costume: undying as the Monster had proved to be, he could hardly have survived the original climactic holocaust totally unscathed. His hair was now burned stubble, exposing unsightly skull-clips, and wrinkled scars marked his cheeks. His suit, shabbier than ever, gained an unaccountable fourteen

'Ware Wolves: Lycanthropy, the curse that brings out the beast in people, was a long time incubating. Universal made *The Werewolf* in 1913 and waited twenty-two years before making another. *Werewolf of London* (1935; *opposite, left*) starred Henry Hull. The makeup by Jack P. Pierce not only influenced that artist's later Chaney *Wolf Man*, but also Michael Landon's teenage version: *I Was a Teenage Werewolf* (American International 1957; *below left*), and Germany's *Lycanthropus* (Royal 1961; *below*). This one was known in England as *I Married a Werewolf* and in America as *Werewolf in a Girls' Dormitory*.

pounds in weight. In his first scene, the Monster's survival in an underground river beneath the ruined mill, Karloff broke a hip.

Bride of Frankenstein (1935) was a sequel, yet it came closer to the original novel than did the original film. It even opened with a prologue based on Mary Shelley's 1817 Preface. Lord Byron (Gavin Gordon) muses over Mary's morality of the Modern Prometheus: 'I relish each separate horror . . . I roll them over on my tongue.' (This allowed four-year-old memories to be refreshed by flashbacks.) He wishes for more and Mary obliges.

From the dying embers of the old mill comes one last belch of flame. 'His insides caught at last!' screeches old Minnie. This crone, a family retainer unseen in the original, is Una O'Connor, a Whale grotesque from *The Invisible Man*. Her mutterings

Living Dolls: Grace Ford was *The Devil Doll* (MGM 1936), looking small against scaled-up sets, an effect Laurel and Hardy pioneered in *Brats* (1930). Grant Williams achieved an atom-age equivalent by performing in front of a back-projection screen: *The Incredible Shrinking Man* (Universal 1957; *left*).

and scuttlings replace those of Dwight Frye: when a great knocking comes upon the castle door, she scurries to answer with an 'All right, don't knock the castle over, we're not all dead yet!' The midnight caller is Dr Pretorius ('Pretorius? There's no sich name!'). This is Ernest Thesiger ('A very queer old gentleman') in a role evolved out of his effeminate Femm. He even says the same line: 'Do you like gin? It is my only weakness.' He brings Frankenstein the result of twenty years' experimentation, artificial life: 'I grew my creatures, like cultures. Grew them as nature does, from seed.' But Pretorius has a size problem: he can only create in miniature. Like a wicked old witch he displays his seven dwarfs in bottles. They range from a lusty Henry VIII (a Whale in-joke: his Bride's real husband – Charles Laughton – won the Oscar as bluff King Hal) to a mermaid ('An experiment with seaweed!').

Meanwhile the Monster seeks shelter in the hut of a blind hermit (O.P.Heggie). It is the burned, spurned brute's first encounter with something other than horror. Accepting him on equal terms as one of nature's cast-offs, the hermit gives the Monster food for body (bread and wine) and soul (Ave Maria on the violin). He teaches him simple words ('Bread, wine') and simple truths ('Friend good, fire bad'), but their fiddle-playing idyll is interrupted when huntsman John Carradine bursts in. In moments the hut is on fire. Whale's symbolism runs amok. Already brought in on a tree in mock crucifixion, now his Monster abandons his God-like friend in a hell of flames and overthrows the statue of a bishop. In the catacombs below, Dr Pretorius is dining off a coffin.

The Monster steps out of the shadows. The sudden sight provokes no fright in Pretorius. He raises a nostril. 'Oh,' he says offhandedly, 'I thought I was alone.' 'Friend?' queries the Monster, and Pretorius gives him the remains of his chicken carcase to crunch. To force Frankenstein's co-operation, Pretorius has the Monster kidnap Elizabeth. Karl (Dwight Frye) is dispatched to obtain a fresh female corpse. (Whale's original plan was to have him kill Elizabeth: the bride of Frankenstein would become the Bride of Frankenstein.) An artificial brain is inserted. The climax comes on a stormy night in a creation so creative that the original *Frankenstein* pales into a pilot. On a table raised on high as Karl flies kites in the lightning sky, the Mate is brought to life under the 'Cosmic Diffuser'. 'The bride of Frankenstein!' pronounces Pretorius as Whale treats us to his trick of curiously-cut closeups of the creature.

There is more mockery in the music: Franz Waxman's excellent score now chimes forth with wedding bells! The Monster reaches beseechingly for his bandaged bride. 'Friend?' he quavers. Her reaction is a sharp screech. 'She hate me, like others,' says the Monster, one tear rolling down one cheek. He pulls a lever and blows the laboratory to pieces, uttering his Famous Last Words: 'We belong dead.'

Bride of Frankenstein remains the biggest-budgeted, best dressed, highest-polished, finest-finished horror film in history; a first-class Hollywood product made with all the artistry and technology a top studio normally lavished upon only its most commercial ventures. It was Whale's best work – and his last in the genre; he felt he could not top it. With it he established himself as the master director of horror – although there are many who feel his sense of humour dilutes rather than enhances the whole. After a period of sad oblivion touched by alcohol and scandal, Whale was found drowned in his own swimming-pool on 29 May 1957.

Chaney was forgotten; Karloff was king; but who could replace Karloff? Laemmle needed a second-string monster; it was bad business to let a star have the whole field to himself. He thought he found one in Henry Hull, silent hero of D.W. Griffith's thriller *One Exciting Night* (1922). Laemmle had Jack Pierce make Hull look so Karloff-like as Magwitch that the posters for *Great Expectations* (1934) boosted that Dickens picture into the horror market. Stuart Walker directed, and when Whale declined further horrors, Laemmle reunited Walker and Hull on *Werewolf of London* (1935).

Valerie Hobson played Lisa to Hull's Wilfred, the unhappy Glendon. Warner Oland, a former Fu Manchu, was Dr Yogami of the University of Carpathia, who bit Dr Glendon one moonlight night. Both were in Tibet at the time, seeking the *mariphasa Lupino lumino*, a flower that blooms in the moon. Its other odd property was that it acted as an antidote to lycanthrobia. Glendon took a cutting back to London and nurtured it beneath a strange lamp, but both he and Yogami needed the prick of its pollen thorn. Yogami wins the race but loses his life, for Glendon grows hairy and kills him. Yogami had warned, 'The werewolf instinctively seeks to kill the thing it loves best.' Now Glendon stalks his wife. The head of Scotland Yard arrives in time to shoot him down and watch as the werewolf changes, in death, to the doctor.

Hull, in a six-hour makeup job (four to put on, two to take off) did well as the werewolf, but was

Fiery Pyres: Gloria Holden as Countess Marya Zaleska, better known as *Dracula's Daughter* (Universal 1936), presides over a private pyre for her father, the late Count (*below*). Kirsten Lindholm in *Twins of Evil* (Hammer 1971) is 'the innocent, beautiful woodman's daughter' who, continues the caption, 'writhes in terror as the flames leap when the fanatical Brotherhood burn her at the stake' (*right*). *Opposite:* Bela Lugosi, undead with a hole in his head to prove it, enfolds Elizabeth Allan in *Mark of the Vampire* (MGM 1935).

too clipped of hair and speech as the hero. His harsh voice and brusque ways robbed the role of sympathy, spoiling Laemmle's hopes of a new Karloff to replace his new Chaney. Laemmle also tried to catch a little Whale: two old cockney biddies called Mrs Moncaster and Mrs Whack cackled eccentrically through the film, but instead of relief they were padding. Robert Harris wrote the story, grafting European folklore to Jekyll and Hyde. Jack Pierce's makeup also recalled that much-filmed monster, especially when, working with John P. Fulton, the dying change from wolf to man was shown as a series of overlapping dissolves.

Karloff, Lugosi and Poe, Universal's triple-threat, were teamed again in *The Raven* (1935). Walker had proved no Whale and this time Laemmle tried Louis Friedlander, who had directed *The Vanishing Shadow*. Lugosi, though as ever billed below, for once led the field as Richard Vollin, plastic surgeon with Poe on the Brain. His house on Hillview Heights was a torture-chamber shrine to the morbid poet. As Edmond Bateman, bearded fugitive from San Quentin, Karloff comes demanding a new face. Lugosi gives him one. He

unveils it in six long mirrors, all of which the snarling Karloff smashes. 'Maybe if a man looks ugly he does ugly things,' Karloff had said. Now he was more than ugly: Lugosi had tampered with his seventh cranial nerve. 'Your monstrous ugliness creates monstrous hate!' jibes Lugosi, 'I can use your hate.' Forced to assist in Lugosi's mad scheme to win Irene Ware by torturing Samuel S. Hinds, Karloff is shot saving her. He explodes the master switchboard and Lugosi dies screaming between in-crushing walls. His stuffed raven falls symbolically to the floor. 'Poe, you are avenged!' cried Lugosi at one climax; others would disagree.

Karloff and Lugosi were matched again in *The Invisible Ray* (1935). They co-starred as doctors Janos Rukh and Felix Benet, but this time Friedlander's serial-style science-fiction made way for Lambert Hillyer's fabulous futurism. The opening is breathtaking. In his laboratory-cum-observatory perched atop a Carpathian mountain, Karloff captures light rays from the past, reconstituting constellations within a great glass dome. A kind of time machine, it takes him beyond Andromeda to track the trajectory of a mysterious meteor. Enrolling Lugosi he treks to Africa to excavate the rock and harness its curious property, Radium-X. This ray cures blindness at short range, melts mountains at long range and makes Karloff glow in the dark. Only Lugosi can supply the antidote. Karloff's brain turns and he goes on a rampage of revenge. His very touch kills, and after each murder he melts a statue of one Deadly Sin (stone symbols surmounting that Universal edifice, Notre Dame). In the end his old mother (Violet Kemble Cooper) dashes the antidote from his fingers for 'breaking the first rule of science'. Karloff bursts into flames, leaps through the window, and goes up in smoke. A set-piece finale to a historic double-act: Karloff and Lugosi would ride again, but never as equal partners.

Universal brought the golden age of horror full circle with a sequel to the story that had started it. Lambert Hillyer directed Gloria Holden, an unknown from London, as Countess Marya Zaleska from Transylvania, otherwise *Dracula's Daughter* (1936). A moon-faced beauty, Hungarian of cheekbone, slumber-lidded of eye, Miss Holden played with sombre restraint as the cursed soul who sought only release. She intoned lines by John Balderston and Garrett Fort with sadness and belief, aided perhaps by some years in radio. Stealing the staked corpse of her father, she presides over his funeral pyre.

Ladies' Night: Women's Lib hits Transylvania. Barbara Shelley (*right*) bares her fangs and etceteras in *Dracula, Prince of Darkness* (Hammer 1965), setting a fashion followed by a female fiend in *The Return of Count Yorga* (American International 1971; *below right*). Ingrid Pitt as *Countess Dracula* (Hammer 1970; *below*) found an ideal cure for old age: virgin's blood. *Opposite page:* Nancy Barrett is crossed in *House of Dark Shadows* (MGM 1970; *top*). A vampire woman was but one horror in Bert I. Gordon's *Saint George and the Seven Curses* (UA 1961; *centre left*). Hammer also contributed Adrienne Corri, who bled Elizabeth Seal in *Vampire Circus* (1972; *bottom left*) and Barbara Shelley again as *The Gorgon* (1964; *bottom right*).

118

'Unto Adoni and Aseroth, into the keeping of the lords of the flame and lower pits, I consign this body, to be for evermore consumed in this purging fire. Let all baleful spirits that threaten the souls of men be banished by the sprinkling of this salt. Be thou exorcized, O Dracula, and thy body long undead, find destruction throughout eternity in the name of thy dark, unholy master. In the name of the all holiest, and through this cross, be the evil spirit cast out until the end of time.'

Her own epitaph is less wordy but more telling. Says old Von Helsing (old Van Sloan), 'She was beautiful when she died – a hundred years ago!' The Countess had expired at the hands of her jealous servant, Sandor (Irving Pichel in black hair and nostrils), shot through the heart by his wooden arrow. It was a fitting funeral for the first Universal epoch.

MGM continued to hold second place in the horror-film race. After three years they finally for-gave *Freaks* and let Tod Browning have his head. *Mark of the Vampire* (1935), a talking version of his *London After Midnight*, switched the locale to Mareka in Czechoslovakia, a more suitable venue for a revamp. One of his writers was Guy Endore, author of the best modern novel on lycanthropy, 'Werewolf of Paris'; his photographer was James Wong Howe; his stars were Lionel Barrymore, Bela Lugosi and Lionel Atwill. Clearly only the best would do. The original Lon Chaney double-role was doubled up: Barrymore as the investigator and Lugosi as the vampire. An additional twist was that Barrymore played in a realistic variation of Chaney's original vampire makeup, a shaggy old scientist called Professor Zelen, while Lugosi played straight Dracula in black cloak and eyeballs as Count Mora. Boosting the cast was the Vampire Girl, blood-sister to America's Panther Woman. Carol Borland, winner of the role of Luna, daughter of Mora, had an unfair edge in that she played with Lugosi on a *Dracula* tour. This had prepared her for almost anything, except Tod Browning. He wanted her

Double Feature: Boris Karloff and Bela Lugosi, the first great stars of horror, became partners in crime. Less the Abbott and Costello of horror films, more your Laurel and Hardy: like those latter-day laughter-makers Lugosi and Karloff were actors of equal weight. However, Karloff quickly took the lead, and by the time of *The Body Snatcher* (RKO 1945; *above*) Lugosi was reduced to small-part support – except in the billing. He fared better in the Universal team-ups, flaying Karloff alive in *The Black Cat* (1934; *opposite*), released in England as *House of Doom*, and tampering with his nerve ends in *The Raven* (1935; *left*).

to swoop bat-like at the window. First they had to design and build a flying harness that would hide beneath her Adrian-designed gowns. A jockey hired as her stand-in got airsick. Her springed bat-wings sprang in instead of out. She had a bar from the back of her neck to her ankles to hold her stiff: when they forgot to lower the tail-wires first her swoop turned into a belly-flop. It took three weeks to shoot a shot that lasted ten seconds; a stunt which, according to the plot, was quickly rigged by actors to scare a murderer. This ultimate exposition was more preposterous than the proposition that 'there are such things'.

Mad Love (1935) was released in England under the title of the novel from which it was taken, *The Hands of Orlac*. Colin Clive continued in nerve-wracked vein as Stephen Orlac, concert pianist, whose famous hands have to be amputated after a train smash. Dr Gogol, bald, bulb-eyed, brilliant, sews on some new ones: hands cut from the corpse of Rollo, a murderous knife-thrower. Gogol dies from a knife thrown by those hands, but not before he has framed Orlac for killing his father and frightened him with an horrendous apparition. Orlac follows a beckoning figure to the Inn of the Three Feathers. It throws back its cloak: its hands are steel. 'I have no hands. Your hands were mine once.' Then it pulls back its cape. 'They cut off my head, but Gogol put it back!': a bloated white face, fixed in place with a leather brace.

There are other joys, some familiar. Orlac's wife is branded nightly in *Grand Guignol* at 'Le Théâtre des Horreurs' (just as the Judge's daughter danced 'The Spirit of Poe' in *The Raven*). Gogol pumps a private organ (as did the Phantom, the Terror, and

Karloff before him), serenading a wax figure of Orlac's wife (an echo of Atwill). His pet cockatoo (a familiar in the tradition of Lugosi's vulture of *White Zombie*) exposes her when she takes the place of the statue, by drawing blood with its claws. 'Each man should kill the thing he loves,' expounds Gogol (*après* Yogami) as he strangles Frances Drake with her own hair.

There was a familiarity about the credits, too: Karl Freund directed (sadly his last such exercise; he returned to his old love, the camera), and John L. Balderston and Guy Endore worked on the screenplay. Unfamiliar, and horridly so, was the star. Peter Lorre from Hungary, the child-like child-killer of *M* (1931), Fritz Lang's first talkie. Lorre's ogling Gogol was the original egg-head with eyes poached to match. His Hollywood debut brought a new face, style and thrill to the horror film.

The Devil Doll (1936) was the last horror film from MGM, and from Tod Browning. It was a tremendous farewell for him, totally fantastic yet completely characteristic. Lionel Barrymore, Devil's Island escapee, donning drag as Madame Mandelip, proprietress of a Montmartre doll shop, was familiar Chaney stuff; novelty lay in making the dolls miniaturized humans. Marcel and Malita, eccentric scientists, devised their diminisher as an answer to the over-population problem, but the cracked ex-con sees wider possibilities. He dispatches his eight-inch automata to wreak revenge on the men who framed him. A brilliant sequence showed Grace Ford as little Lachna, stirring to life in the crook of sleeping Juanita Quigley's arm, climbing down the eiderdown, squeezing through an ajar door, shinning up a chair-leg, tossing pearls down to the waiting Barrymore, and running a poisoned stiletto into the outflung arm of snoring Robert Greig.

Browning took his plot from 'Burn Witch Burn', a novel by Abraham Merritt. He threw out the author's alchemy and had Guy Endore, Garrett Fort and Erich Von Stroheim switch the script to science-fiction. Learning from his last over-explained vampires, Browning let his pictures carry conviction by simply looking real. It was an incredible climax to an incredible career. When Browning died in 1962, he had been so long in the wilderness that Hollywood was surprised to learn he had still been alive.

Hands Down: Colin Clive in *Mad Love* (MGM 1935; *above*); Lon Chaney Jr as *The Wolf Man* (Universal 1941).

'Even a man who is pure in heart,
And says his prayers by night,
May become a wolf when the wolfbane blooms
And the Autumn moon is bright.'

It wasn't so much the moon that turned Lon Chaney into *The Wolf Man* (1941), or even a bite from Bela Lugosi. It was a six-hour sit in the make-up chair while Jack Pierce painstakingly pasted him over with yak-hair and stranded kelp. Wearing a T-shaped nosepiece of moulded rubber, fangs on his teeth, hair in his palms, and feet tippy-toed into padded paws, Chaney knew what it was to suffer the curse of the pentagram. Small wonder Evelyn Ankers screamed at the sight, so frightfully well that this Chile-born English lass became the second First Lady of Horror, finally tucking more monster movies under her girdle than even Fay Wray. But Pierce's processing was only the beginning of Chaney's ordeal. Worse even than the nightly eat-off with acetone was the great transformation scene organized by Pierce, Fulton, and Joseph Valentine the photographer.

'The day we did the transformations I came in at two a.m. When I hit that position they would take little nails and drive them through the skin at the edge of my fingers, on both hands, so that I wouldn't move them any more. While I was in this position they would build a plaster cast of the back of my head. Then they would take the drapes from behind me and starch them, and while they were drying them, they would take the camera and weigh it down with one ton, so that it wouldn't quiver when people walked. They had targets for my eyes up there. Then, while I'm still in this position, they would shoot five or ten frames of film in the camera. They'd take that film out and send it to the lab. While it was there the makeup man would come and take the whole thing off my face, and put on a new one, only less. I'm still immobile. When the film came back from the lab they'd put it back in the camera and then they'd check me. They'd say, "Your eyes have moved a little bit, move them to the right . . . now your shoulder is up. . . ." Then they'd roll it again and shoot another ten frames. Well, we did twenty-one changes of makeup and it took twenty-two hours. I won't discuss about the bathroom!'

Yet for all that, Chaney loved his Wolf Man: 'He was my baby!' Although an unlikely choice for an English heir (he plays Lawrence Stewart, son of Sir John Talbot of Llanwelly, Wales), with an unlikely star for a father (Chaney towered a good foot over Claude Rains), he did the double in the best Jekyll and Hyde tradition. *The Wolf Man*, a title originally announced for Karloff in 1932, sprang from the monster makeup of *Werewolf of London*. It also had that film's plot twist of the two werewolves. Lugosi, aptly cast as Bela, played the biter, but Chaney soon killed him with his silver-handled cane. Maleva the mother who crooned the rune had more to say, over her son's corpse, and over Larry's later. 'The way you walk is thorny through no fault of your own. For as the rain enters the soil, and evil enters the sea, so tears run to their predestined end. Your suffering is over. Now find peace for eternity, my son.' Fine words, written by Curt Siodmak, intoned by an ex-star of the Moscow Art Theatre, Madame Maria Ouspenskaya. But they still failed to end Chaney's suffering.

'They cast me as the Frankenstein Monster. It took four hours to make me up. Then they led me to the set. They dug a hole in the cliff and put me in. They stuck a straw in my mouth and covered me up with cement. It took till twelve o'clock to

Rise and Shine: Charles Laughton in *The Hunchback of Notre Dame* (RKO 1939; *above*); *The Mummy* (Universal 1932).

It comes to Life !

CARL LAEMMLE *presents*

KARLOFF
THE UNCANNY
in

"The MUMMY"

TRADE SHOW:
(and for heaven's sake—and your
own—don't miss it!)
WEDNESDAY, JAN. II
PRINCE EDWARD THEATRE, at 8.30 p.m.

 A UNIVERSAL PICTURE

KONG
by Edgar Wallace

THE STRANGEST STORY EVER CONCEIVED BY MAN
A Merian C. Cooper - Ernest Schoedsack Production

EVEN MIGHTIER THAN "KING KONG"!

GAPPA

THE TRIPHIBIAN MONSTER
EASTMAN COLOUR 'SCOPE

get me sealed in. Then everybody went to lunch!'

The Ghost of Frankenstein (1942) was released on Friday the 13th, a lucky day for Universal. The picture had been a great gamble. Karloff had forsworn the Monster for mad doctor roles more in keeping with his advancing dignity; Basil Rathbone was now totally identified as the movies' Sherlock Holmes. Rathbone's role of Wolf was rewritten for Sir Cedric Hardwicke and called Ludwig, Frankenstein's second son and Doctor of the Mind.

Karloff's Monster remained unchanged, except by Chaney. Jack Pierce tried to mould him into a Karloff, but the taller, thicker, jowlier man remained a hulking Lennie, a flat-topped, jut-browed brute of a mute. His performance has robotic power, but lacks soul, even a man-made one.

Monster Posters: *King Kong* was still called *Kong* when RKO first advertised it in January 1933, and was still the mighty yardstick when Nikkatsu advertised *Gappa* in 1967. *Above*, the first coupling of *Dracula* and *Frankenstein* in 1938.

The story starts where *Son* leaves off as Dwight Frye dynamites the Frankenstein castle. Rising from the ruins comes, inexplicably, Ygor (Lugosi). He excavates the Monster from his pit of sulphur. Last seen bubbling at 800 degrees, the stuff is now as dry as dust. In a splendid scene the stumbling Monster renews his strength in a storm: his mother, the lightning, strikes at his neck electrodes. Then it's off for Vasaria and Dr Ludwig, whose determination to dissect the Monster is undone by a visitation from his father's ghost: 'Would you destroy that which I dedicated my life to creating? Unknowingly I gave it a criminal brain. With your knowledge of science you can cure that.' Inspired, Ludwig plans to transplant the brain of the late kindly Dr Kettering. But he reckons without Ygor, who has found an evil soulmate in Ludwig's assistant, Lionel Atwill. When the Monster revives on the operating table he speaks with Ygor's voice: 'I have the strength of a hundred men! I, Ygor, will live for ever!' Ludwig is horrified: 'The crime of my father is now mine, but a thousandfold!' he cries as the Monster thrashes around the laboratory. But nature prevails: the Monster goes blind. 'What good is a brain without eyes?' he screams, flinging Atwill into a generator. The lab roars into flames, a beam falls on the Monster, his face begins to blister, and Ralph Bellamy speedily escorts Evelyn Ankers towards the rising sun.

'The New Master Character Creator', as Chaney was billed, was promptly put under wraps: the 400 yards of tattered gauze vacated by Tom Tyler. Chaney was so painted over by Pierce with liquidized Fuller's Earth, so caked with cracked beauty clay, that even a High Priest of Karnak would have been hard put to tell the difference. Kharis, who last went to blazes in overturned oil, limped unsinged in *The Mummy's Tomb* (1942), animated as much by the call of the box office as by the juice of the tana leaves. The film was short on thrills but long on economy: Pierce fashioned a mask that saved a deal of makeup time. It also helped stuntman Edwin Parker look like Chaney look like Tyler look like Karloff, for once again the Waters of Khar unfold with their flashbacks. This time they take in clips from *The Mummy's Hand*, too, as George Zucco passes on the tana leaves to Turhan Bey. Thirty years have elapsed since that last outing, and this time Kharis turns up in Mapleton, Massachusetts, to bring the anger of the Ancient Gods upon the greying Dick Foran. Turhan Bey's plan to enrol lovely Elyse Knox as his Priestess is foiled by fire: the village mob with

Monsters Meet: Boris Karloff, too old to wear the makeup, came face to face with himself in *House of Frankenstein* (Universal 1944; *right*). Glenn Strange, a B-western 'heavy', wore an adaptation of Jack Pierce's original Karloffian conception. Found frozen (*below*), Strange later survived a climatic quicksand to be revived again in *House of Dracula* (Universal 1945; *below right*). He failed to survive his obligatory encounter with Abbott and Costello.

their flaming torches is a familiar climax – spliced in from *Frankenstein*! Chaney, who hated his Mummy as much as he loved his Baby, unwound by playing Larry Talbot again.

Frankenstein Meets the Wolf Man (1942) was conceived as a battle of the giants. The idea was vintage Laemmle: instead of teaming stars, team monsters. But Universal had set themselves a problem; both the Frankenstein Monster and the Wolf Man had last been played by the same actor, Lon Chaney. Chaney would let no one else play his Baby, so who to cast for the Monster? The problem was soon solved. Lugosi's part in the saga, Ygor, was now dead, his brain in the Monster's head, his voice in the Monster's mouth. What more natural than have Lugosi play the Monster? If he was still recognizable under Pierce's makeup, then that was simply Ygor showing through! Besides, there was an element of destiny that the fans would not have forgotten. Lugosi had rejected the original role twelve years earlier. Lugosi could no longer afford to be so choosy. He brought to the Monster his own curious interpretation, a hissing evil that snarled through the makeup. His stretch-armed strutting seems senseless in context, yet was not so in shooting. For as filmed Lugosi's Monster is blind as a bat. Pre-release shortening by the studio removed the reason for Lugosi's climactic close-upped smile: Patric Knowles has not only restored the Monster's strength, but his sight, too!

Larry Talbot finds the Monster entombed in ice beneath the ruins of Frankenstein's home in Vasaria. The Wolf Man has wended from Wales in care of old Maleva, hopeful that the late scientist's records may reveal a release. His curse has apparently overcome the permanent death dealt him by Claude Rains and his silver-headed cane. Baroness Elsa (Ilona Massey replacing Evelyn Ankers), to thwart Patric Knowles' plan, pulls a well-remembered lever. The apparatus explodes, the Monster goes berserk, the werewolf changes, the villagers blast the dam, the young couple flee, the water crashes down, and the castle caves in. That left Chaney, the Universal Monster, one to go for full house.

Son of Dracula (1943) saw Chaney with no make-up other than a moustache, a relaxing change. But his well-fed face was out of place in an undead vampire who lived on blood. Quick-witted J. Edward Bromberg unravels the anagrammatical Anthony Alucard, newly arrived from Budapest as guest of Louise Allbritton, heiress to the Louisiana plantation of Dark Oaks. Metaphysic-

ally minded, she is soon under his spell, and if it hadn't been for Robert Paige finding the Count's coffin down a drain, Evelyn Ankers would have been bitten, too. Curt Siodmak, who had fathered Chaney's Baby, wrote this one, and brought along his brother to direct. In his three-week schedule, Robert Siodmak found time to visualize one nice touch: Alucard's coffin bobs to the surface of a lagoon, the vampire materializes from smoke within, and glides to shore in this spooky punt.

For Chaney the vacation was over. In 1944 it was back to the bandages, twice. *The Mummy's Ghost* had Zucco back with the flashbacks as John Carradine took over the High Priesthood of Arkan (anagrams were in fashion). The mummy of Princess Ananka is on show at the Mapleton Museum. One touch from her devoted Kharis and she crumbles away. Her soul has been reincarnated in Amina El Harun, a local girl. Kharis abducts her for embalming, but Carradine tries to tempt her into tasting the tana leaves. Kharis kills Carradine and stomps off with his girl. Ananka, like Ayesha of old, ages rapidly and the eternal lovers sink blissfully into a swamp.

The Mummy's Curse (1944) was released eight months later yet begins '25 years later!' Peter Coe is the new High Priest and he has a familiar tale to tell Martin Kosleck. The swamp has been drained and Kharis is back on the tana leaves. Ananka has also emerged, this time as Virginia Christine. Kharis carries her off to an abandoned monastery, which he promptly brings down upon everybody's heads. It was the end of a saga, if not of an era. Yet that, too, was closer than either Chaney or Universal thought.

'All Together! The Screen's Titans of Terror!' There could be no complaints about that catchline for *House of Frankenstein* (1944). Curt Siodmak's script reunited the Monster and the Wolf Man, revived Dracula, and more: it brought back Boris Karloff. With other stalwarts of the form in smaller roles, J. Carrol Naish as an evil hunchback, Lionel Atwill as Inspector Arnz, even George Zucco, the film only missed on one count: Bela Lugosi. Dracula went to long John Carradine, a superbly spoken fellow far more cadaverous than his 'son'. Continuity went astray for him, for when last seen Dracula was being cremated at Whitby. Now he materialized upon his skeleton in Zucco's Chamber of Horrors, in top hat, white tie and tails. He also flapped into an outsize bat, animated by John P. Fulton, and died at dawn, reaching for his coffin as the sun dissolved the flesh from his bones.

Monster Funsters: The Frankenstein Monster was created by Universal, survived because of Universal, and continues to survive despite Universal. Edwin Parker first played him for laughs in *Hellzapoppin'* (1941; *opposite top left*), and Glenn Strange caught mermaid Ann Blyth (*opposite below*) on the set of *Abbott and Costello Meet Frankenstein* (1948; *opposite top right*). Lou Costello met both Monster and Dracula in *Abbott and Costello Meet Dr Jekyll and Mr Hyde* (1953), and ultimately Universal cast Fred Gwynne in the Karloff mould for *Munster Go Home* (1966). Yvonne De Carlo was Lily to Fred's Herman (*right*).

Bud **ABBOTT** & Lou **COSTELLO**
MEET DR. JEKYLL & MR. HYDE

CO-STARRING
BORIS KARLOFF   CERT. X

A UNIVERSAL-INTERNATIONAL PICTURE   G.F.D. RELEASE

Karloff was the prime mover as Dr Gustav Niemann, animal experimenter, escaping from Neustadt jail to find Wolf Man and Monster ('Triumphant climax of Frankenstein's genius!') deep-frozen beneath the ruins. First to be thawed is an ungrateful Chaney. 'Neath the light of the full moon he changes again and is suitably shot with a silver bullet 'fired by the hand of one who loves him' (Elena Verdugo). The Monster is climactically revived by Niemann and his 100,000 megavolts. The flashing this requires brings the villagers out with their flaming torches, and they chase him into a handy bog.

The new Monster, the fourth, might have been Lane Chandler, a Western heavy on the Universal payroll. Instead his pardner got the job when Jack Pierce found a more suitable facial contour on Glenn Strange. This big fellow, once a wolfman himself in *The Mad Monster* (1941), had little to offer the role beyond his contour. But he had the world's best teacher by his side.

'Nobody ever helped anybody as much as Boris Karloff helped me. I never forget that. I asked him for advice because I wanted to do this thing as near as he did. He would stay on the set and coach me on the walk and the movements and so forth.'

143

Have pity for Lawrence Stewart Talbot, reluctant werewolf. He sought blessed rest and found none. Universal legend decreed that holy silver would bring death, but Universal Studio legend was a law unto itself. Dr Franz Edelmann was summoned to Vasaria Prison by Inspector Holz (Lionel Atwill). There in a cell stood mad Larry, moonlight in his eyes, yak-hair on his cheeks. Edelmann, whose creed was 'Science against sorcery', took Talbot to his castle laboratory for examination.

'His physical processes give way to self-hypnotism. His glands generate certain hormones which bring about the physical changes. There is a crowding of the brain because the cranial cavity failed to enlarge sufficiently.'

Edelmann cures Larry's lycanthropy by using a home-grown mould to soften and reshape his cranium. Edelmann had a cure for vampirism, too, an antibody to consume the strange parasites he isolated in Dracula's blood. Carradine was back for the Count in *House of Dracula* (1945), his coffin secreted in Edelmann's cellar. Unfortunately Edelmann's blood-transfusion backfires and he gets a dose of the parasites. Unlike the gentlemanly Dracula (who becomes bones in the sun again) Edelmann turns into a fiendish vampire, laughing as he revives the Monster, found dormant in the Devil's Hole. Larry shoots Edelmann, the lab catches fire, and the Monster is hit on the head by his third beam. Tighter scripted than the previous pot-pourri, Edward T. Lowe intertwining the devil's brood where Curt Siodmak had opted for episodes, the film created an excellent new character in the Jekyll/Hyde fiend of Onslow Stevens. Yet it missed something: sincerity perhaps? love perhaps? Karloff perhaps?

Glenn Strange strode again in what proved to be Jack Pierce's last monster makeup.

'When I had the makeup on I had trouble seeing, because the Monster's eyelids hung over my eyes. The makeup made my face raw. The skull cap I wore was so tight it wouldn't let the perspiration out. After a couple of hours I could shake my head and the water would rattle round inside.'

The rattle Strange heard was a death rattle. *House of Dracula* was the last of its line, the end of the Second Generation of the horror film. Not a Golden Age, perhaps a Silver Bullet Age, certainly a Universal Age. The Old Gods put their unholy five out to pasture, Dracula, Monster, Mummy, Wolfman, Invisible Man: Chaney had played them all but one. Like true immortals they would rise again, but as shadows of their former glory. The comeback would come, but it would be just for fun.

Side By Side: Jon Hall took a day off when this still was shot for *Invisible Agent* (Universal 1942; *top*). *The Man In Half Moon Street* (Paramount 1944; *centre*) was Nils Asther, whose age suddenly caught up with him. The surprise of Helen Walker was nothing to the shock of Hazel Court when the same thing happened to Anton Diffring (*bottom*): *The Man Who Could Cheat Death* (1959) was a Hammer film. *Opposite:* corruption keeps Hurd Hatfield young but ages his portrait: *The Picture of Dorian Gray* (MGM 1945).

THE CURSE OF T

**In which Karloff takes his mad
money, Cat People take over, a**

The German horror film had been cursed by the *doppelgänger*; the American horror film was cursed by the Double Bill. Every big picture had to have a little picture in support. Every 'A' must have its 'B': it was a Hollywood law as immutable as any of Amon-Ra's. And when the major studios couldn't make enough 'B's of their own, the minors rushed in and filled the bill. Soon the horror film became as regular on the release roster as the mystery or the Western, with characters as predictable as Charlie Chan or the Bowery Boys.

'Greater than *Frankenstein* say the critics!' They said it, apparently, of *The Monster Walks* (1932), but Mayfair Pictures carefully named no names. The first of the 'B's, this was also the first of the 'H''B's: blue-pencilled by the British Censor until he had introduced his Horror Certificate. Dated in style to start with, by then the poor little picture was so passé that the conscience-stricken distributor retitled it *The Monster Walked*. Hanns Krug, maniac, binding a scientist's daughter to a post, lashing Yogi the Ape to a fury, and strangling his own mother by mistake, brought laughs, some of them unwitting. Clutching Hanns was played by Mischa Auer, who in the years between had changed his line to mad Russians of a different bent.

Bela Lugosi had been the first modern horror star, and he was the first to be cursed by the 'B' people. In 1933 Harry Cohn's Columbia studio was less than major. They made their 'A' pictures in three weeks, and a *Night of Terror* (1933) was scarcely 'A'. Still, it had Lugosi, which is more than Columbia could say for their next, *The Ninth Guest* (1934).

Boris Karloff, too, felt the sting of the 'B's, but by the time he clocked in at Columbia there was a little more honey to be had. *The Black Room* (1935) was almost an 'A', by Columbia's standards at any rate. Karloff in costume played good-and-bad twins, which stretched his talent but not the budget. It was at Columbia, later, that Karloff starred as *The Man They Could Not Hang* (1939), a quickie

Present Arms: Jean Cocteau's fantastic image of living limbs, used in *Beauty and the Beast* (1945), is handed down through the horror film. The clutching hands of Karloff's *Bedlam* (RKO 1946; *below*) match the sawn-off sword-arms of *Jack the Giant Killer* (Small 1961; *right*).

minutes of them at the hands of the censor. Then they sent it out as *Behind the Door*. Found frozen in an ice chamber on Crater Island, Karloff is thawed from his ten-year deep-freeze, living proof that 'frozen therapy' cures cancer. Unhappily, unbelievers unhinge him and he has to be shot. Karloff turns his notes over to Roger Pryor and dies, 'happy in the consciousness that his great labour will be carried on'. But it was a case of carry on Karloff. As Dr John Garth he was back in the Columbia laboratory, seeking a 'cure for death'. This time the title was *Before I Hang* (1940). A serum of human blood, injected direct into the heart, restores the twinkle to Karloff's rheumy eye. Unfortunately it was murderer's blood, so Karloff becomes not only younger, but a strangler to boot. Luckily, Bruce Bennett arrives in time to save Evelyn Keyes for better things.

The Devil Commands (1941) had better things for Karloff: a new director, Edward Dmytryk, and a good book as a basis, 'The Edge of Running Water' by William Sloane. Karloff was Dr Julian Blair who, stormbound in his private power-station, harnessed the living to link with the dead. He failed, but not so badly as the censor's scissors led the British to believe. *The Boogie Man Will Get You* (1942) teamed Karloff with Peter Lorre as Nathaniel Billings and Dr Lorentz. They sent up the series by failing to create an electrical superman out of Slapsie Maxie Rosenbloom. Karloff ended his contract with a smile. It was the last of the medicos.

The Return of the Vampire (1943) was the return of Lugosi. Columbia did the old Count well by casting him as Armand Tesla of Rumania, revived in the London Blitz when Nazi bombs disturb his grave. Workmen mistake the stake in his heart for shrapnel and extract it. Soon he is back in action, fanging Nina Foch, turning Matt Willis into a hairy werewolf, and generally bedevilling Frieda Inescort. Willis rebels and drags the vampire into the sun. A waxen image of Lugosi, moulded over a skeleton, gradually melted: a careful climax completely cut from the British print, despite the censor's award of an 'H'. He had less problems with *Cry of the Werewolf* (1944), in which Nina Foch switched sides. As Celeste La Tour, Queen of the Trioga gypsies, she inherited the crown and the curse from her mother. No shape in wolf's clothing, Miss Foch turned into the real thing: an off-screen transformation upon which film fan frowned but censor smiled. He gave it an 'A'.

So Columbia finished with monsters; but the corpse of the horror film, revived in their laboratory, went stomping on. In a new direction, down Poverty Row. With a Mad Doctor in charge, all a small studio needed was a little sparky spectacle in the way of stock electrical gadgetry and some low-key lighting (an appealing economy in itself).

Karloff still had his standards: Monogram, yes; PRC no. When Karloff turned down a script from the smaller studios, there was always Lugosi. 'Ecksss-ellent!' he would invariably exclaim as he went about his, and their, fiendish work, happy to take the money and lope.

Karloff was happy enough to make *The Ape* (1940) for Monogram, an Adam Hull Shirk play the firm had filmed as *The House of Mystery* (1934). William Nigh had directed then, and directed again, but could hardly have recognized Curt Siodmak's adaptation. Karloff killed an escaped ape, skinned it, and hid in the hide to ambush villagers and extract their spinal fluid. It was all in a good cause: a cure for paralysis. It was easy work for Karloff, too. Not only could he act mad doctors on his head, once in the ape-suit a double took over! Lugosi clearly took over in the case of *The Devil Bat* (1940): his Dracula tones and suspect sneer hardly fitted the role of 'kindly physician, Paul Carruthers'. In the rushed world of the B-picture there was seldom time for a re-write. This PRC piece had Lugosi creating electrically-enlarged bats, trained to attack anyone wearing Lugosi's lotion, a sinister after-shave. He died by his own bat. Yet for all that, six years later when Rosemary La Planche came to town as *Devil Bat's Daughter* (1946), her fears of 'inherited vampirism' were exposed as the mere machination of a jealous psychiatrist. Worse, she cleared her father's name in as blatant a whitewash job as was ever conceived by Tom Sawyer.

Lugosi made nine 'B's for Monogram, all of them for a kind of sub-section called Banner Pictures, a 'B' studio's 'B' unit. It was run by Sam Katzman, an ex-prop boy. The films made money, but little sense. *The Invisible Ghost* (1941) had Lugosi as Charles Kessler, who had only to see his wife's face at the window to turn into a stalking strangler. Why was never explained; nor was there a ghost – unless it was truly invisible. *Spooks Run Wild* (1941) put Lugosi among the East Side Kids: juvenile capers written by a young Carl Foreman. *Black Dragons* (1942) had Lugosi giving plastic surgery to Japanese spies. *The Corpse Vanishes* (1942) was shown in England as *The Case of the Missing Brides*. Lugosi was Dr Lorentz, luring ladies from the altar with a whiff of his orchid, and keeping the corpse of his wife alive with their virgin blood.

Bowery at Midnight (1942) saw Lugosi doubling up. By day he is Professor Brenner, slum missioner; by night, Karl Wagner, with a more sinister mission: crime. He is duly done away with by a cellarful of living dead.

The Ape Man (1943), called *Lock Your Doors* in England, had Lugosi as Karloff: or so internal evidence would suggest. It was scripted from an original called 'They Creep in the Dark' by Karl Brown, who had written the Columbia Karloffs. It was made at a time when Karloff was too busy on stage in 'Arsenic and Old Lace' to complete his Columbia contract. Odder: in that play Karloff played Jonathan Brewster, and in this film Lugosi played James Brewster – a pretty strange name for a Hungarian. The plot itself is uncommonly like *The Ape*, which Karloff had appeared in for Monogram. Lugosi kills people to obtain supplies of fresh spinal fluid, the only antidote to his apishness. The twist is that instead of donning a gorilla skin, Lugosi is half-gorilla himself.

Ghosts on the Loose (1943) was Lugosi and the East Side Kids again. This time the British called it *Ghosts in the Night*: a rare case of trying to make a film sound more horrific than it was. *The Voodoo Man* (1944) was an all-star movie by Monogram standards: Lugosi, Zucco and Carradine as Marlow, Nicholas and Job, zombie-makers. The unwholesome three were reunited in *Return of the Ape Man* (1944). This catch-penny piece had nothing at all to do with the previous year's success. It justified its title by being about the return of an apeman. Lugosi as Professor Dexter revives prehistoric Frank Moran from an Arctic iceberg. He inserts

Double Exposed: Boris Karloff, usually a subject for the makeup man (*The Man With Nine Lives*: Columbia 1940; *opposite*), was double-exposed for *The Walking Dead* (Warner 1936; *above left*). George Zucco co-starred with George Zucco in *Dead Men Walk* (PRC 1943; *above*).

John Carradine's brain and the apeman turns into George Zucco! The logic was frightening if the film was not.

Of all the 'B' movie monsters, the zombie was favourite. The walking dead looked pretty much like the walking quick, particularly if you used the less expressive, hence less expensive actors. Besides, a zombie cannot talk and that was another saving: the union scale was lower for a non-speaking part!

The Halperin Brothers, who had started things off with *White Zombie* (1932), dug them up again four years later for *Revolt of the Zombies* (1936). Whilst steamy Cambodia stood in nicely for shadowy Haiti, keen Dean Jagger was no replacement for Lugosi. Nor were his squad of zombie soldiers dead ringers for Legendre's Angels of Death, even if they did march implacably through shot and shell: truly impenetrable Orientals. Yet they were better by far than Dr Sangre and his Caribbean corpses in Monogram's *King of the Zombies* (1941). Henry Victor, once a hero in British silent films, played the Voodoo sorcerer in a style that, at least, proved his consistency. *Revenge of the Zombies* (1943) starred John Carradine as Dr Von Altmann, Nazi scientist, operating out of a Louisiana manse. Here he is building a zombie army for the Führer, starting with his wife. Lila the lady

151

Face to Face: Rondo Hatton was the only horror film star to play monsters without makeup. Cast as 'The Creeper' he appeared in *House of Horrors* (Universal 1946; *above*). Hatton suffered from acromegaly, a distorting disease simulated by Ralph Morgan in *The Monster Maker* (PRC 1944; *opposite above*), Leo G. Carroll in *Tarantula* (Universal 1955; *right*) and Michael Brennan in *Doomwatch* (Tigon 1972; *page 155*). Even more frightening were the faces worn by George Sawaya in *The Black Sleep* (Bel Air 1956; *above right*), Herbert Lom in *Murders in the Rue Morgue* (American International 1971; *opposite below left*), and Philip Coolidge in William Castle's *The Tingler* (Columbia 1959; *opposite below right*).

zombie was played in the manner born by Veda Ann Borg. The British distributor, having called *The Corpse Vanishes – The Case of the Missing Brides*, called *Revenge of the Zombies – The Corpse Vanished*! Carradine, borne into a bayou by Miss Borg, was back in a trice as Professor Randolph. In *Face of Marble* (1945) he restored life of a kind to a drowned sailor, his own deranged wife, and a Great Dane. They kill him. It was the last of the Monograms.

PRC, or to give them their due, the Producers Releasing Corporation, was to Monogram what Monogram was to Columbia. PRC's Sam Katzman was called Sigmund Neufeld, who formed a curiously harmonious partnership with Sam Newfield. Together this team found time between Westerns to produce and direct a field of four. George Zucco was their biggest name. He played in three but made up for it by playing in one twice. A star on the PRC lot, Zucco was a small-part fellow elsewhere, lending his Manchester lip-roll and his marbly eyeballs to many a creepy cameo. In *The Mad Monster* (1942) he was Dr Lorenzo Cameron, growing hair on his handyman with transfusions of wolf's blood. Pedro the simpleton was an initiation into horror for Glenn Strange, former wrestler,

would-be Monster. Zucco's preposterous proposition that infusions of living wolf's blood could create an invincible army was scoffed at by the ghostly conclave of scientists summoned up in his crazed brain. Yet someone did take him seriously, the British censor. *The Mad Monster* was banned for twelve years and only then allowed out with an 'X' Certificate, the Adults Only ticket that ultimately replaced the 'H'. Even then they insisted that every cinema exhibiting the film must also exhibit this notice: 'The public would be quite mistaken to think that any personal characteristics could be passed on by blood transfusion. Animal blood is never used for transfusions in the treatment of disease.' So there.

Dead Men Walk (1942) was Zucco's *doppelgänger*. He appeared as Dr Harold Clayton and disappeared as his twin brother Elwyn. This vampire was assisted by Zolarr, a hunchbacked comeback for Dwight Frye, who promptly went away again. *The Monster Maker* (1944) was Dr Igor Markov, played by J. Carrol Naish for a change. Not a nice one, for in order to wreak his will upon Wanda McKay he injected her father with acromegaly. As he was a concert pianist the resultant swellings hurt his career as much as they did him. A nasty piece by any standards, even PRC's. Zucco returned for a less than grand finale, *The Flying Serpent* (1946). As Professor André Forbes, archaeologist, he stumbles upon Montezuma's treasure. It is guarded by a fierce feathered reptile, so Zucco trains it to kill. It drinks the blood of anyone upon whom Zucco plants its feather. And if the proceedings sound familiar, remember Lugosi and his Devil Bat.

Republic Pictures came first in the minor league studios, but last in the horror field. Herbert J. Yates had more interest in Rogers and Trigger than Boris and Bela. He had even more interest in Vera Hruba Ralston, his regular star. He married her, but not before he had starred her in one of the title roles of *The Lady and the Monster* (1944). The British censor, shocked, changed that to *The Lady and the Doctor*. Later Republic changed it to *The Tiger Man*. Playing the role of Monster/Doctor/Tiger Man was Erich Von Stroheim, 'The Man you Love to Hate'. As Professor Franz Mueller, 'a diabolical and self-centred scientist', he extracted the brain of a fresh-dead financier and kept it alive in a bowl. It grew to dominate Richard Arlen. Curt

Bat Trick: Bela Lugosi in *The Devil Bat* (PRC 1940; *above*); *Doomwatch* (Tigon 1972).

Siodmak's novel 'Donovan's Brain', was more sincerely served by later remakes.

The Phantom Speaks (1945) was similar stuff: Richard Arlen was in it, but he was not the one possessed. Stanley Ridges was the psycho-scientist taken over by the vengeful soul of an executed killer. Tom Powers was seen in double-exposure, but not in Britain, where the film was banned. *The Vampire's Ghost* (1945) meant brief stardom for John Abbott, a sad-eyed, bag-eyed soul from the small-part ranks. He played Webb Fallon, who ran the honky-tonk in Bakunda, West Africa, and turned out to be a vampire, cursed in the days of Queen Elizabeth. *Valley of the Zombies* (1946) was another promotion: Ian Keith, needing fresh blood to maintain his immortality, rejoiced under the name of Ormand Murks. *The Catman of Paris* (1945) was Robert Wilke in whiskers, but despite a starrier support (Carl Esmond and Leonore Aubert), like Ormand Murks he, too, failed to make it to England.

Of the major studios who ran their own 'B' picture units, Warner Brothers-First National were quick off the mark with *The Return of the Terror* (1934), a rejig of that very first horror talkie. They used the same gimmick for *The Return of Dr X* (1939), but Humphrey Bogart could hardly be considered a dead ringer for Lionel Atwill, even with a becoming white stripe in his hair. The film itself seemed in need of a transfusion: it was shown in sepia. *Sh! The Octopus* (1937) was a comedy workover for *The Gorilla* – which had been a comedy to start with – but the British censor failed to see anything funny in *The Mysterious Doctor* (1943), and gave it an 'H' for its headless ghost. Perhaps the final disclosure that it was actually a Nazi, trying to stop our brave Cornish villagers from working a tin mine, proved too much to bear.

Paramount's only 'B'-class horror was *The Monster and the Girl* (1941), a rescoring of a 1920 silent called *Go and Get It*. This time Philip Terry was the executed murderer whose brain, inserted into an ape by George Zucco, impelled the beast's vengeful rampage.

Twentieth Century-Fox scored but two, but two good ones. The better came first. *The Undying Monster* (1942) was directed by John Brahm, a Hamburger who had changed his name from Hans. Taken from Jessie Douglas Kerruish's good 1936 novel, the tale of a family cursed since the Crusades

Hands Up: *The Return of Count Yorga* (AIP 1971; *opposite above*); *Dracula AD 1972* (Hammer 1972). *Right:* Bela Lugosi in *Black Dragons* (PRC 1942).

was moody stuff, quite spoilt by the British censor's scissors. Not only did he remove the carefully-photographed final metamorphosis, leaving audiences to wonder why the dim thing that the police shot should suddenly look like John Howard, but he also insisted on the title being changed to *The Hammond Mystery*. Fortunately enough of Brahm's brilliance was devoted to less shocking sequences so that most of his mood remained. Lucien Ballard swung his camera round an ancient room, alighting on odd objects at each dour bong of midnight. Casting and Cornish atmosphere were both good, too, perhaps because Brahm did his first film work at Twickenham studios. Only one thing spoiled the script. The rune, obligatory to any werewolf film, ran:

'When the stars are bright on a frosty night,
Beware the baying in the rocky lane.'

To film fans there was only one Rocky Lane: the Republic Western star!

Fox's other film was *Dr Renault's Secret* (1942). Fox's secret was that this was really *The Wizard* all over again (and that had been *Balaoo*). George Zucco played the French doctor who proved Darwin was right by operating upon an ape. J. Carrol Naish was the end-product, alias Noel the handyman from Java. He died, as did they all, saving the doctor's daughter from abductive Mike Mazurki. The director was artistic Harry Lachman.

RKO Radio had a 'B' picture unit that was a different belfry of bats: Charles Koerner, production chief, organized it purely to produce horror films. In charge he placed a Russian-born journalist who

'B' Beings: J. Carrol Naish came in handy as the apeman-servant of *Dr Renault's Secret* (Twentieth Century-Fox 1942; *right*), and that latter-day Frankenstein Glenn Strange had a dry run as *The Mad Monster* (PRC 1941; *below*). Bela Lugosi and John Carradine seem as bewildered as neanderthal George Zucco in *Return of the Ape Man* (PRC 1944; *opposite centre*), a sequel in name only to *The Ape Man* (PRC 1943; *opposite below left*). Lugosi alone was in that, while Carradine made a lady out of Acquanetta the Ape Woman in *Captive Wild Woman* (Universal 1943; *opposite top and bottom right*), with a little help from Jack P. Pierce and his yak-hair.

Cheap Horrors: The cheapest horror pictures not only skimped on budgets, they cheated on chills, too. *The Strange Case of Dr RX* (Universal 1942) billed top monster Lionel Atwill (*below*) but he was only a red herring called Dr Fish. The ape and girl still (*opposite*) was featured big in the publicity but never appeared in the film. *The Return of Dr X* (Warner 1939) had as much to do with their well-remembered monstrosity *Dr X* as *The Return of the Ape Man* had to do with *The Ape Man*. But it did have Humphrey Bogart (*left*).

had been David O. Selznick's story editor. Vladimir Ivan Lewton, who called himself Val, was given his first assignment, a title created by Koerner, pre-tested and found audience-appealing. Out of *Cat People* (1942) Lewton wrought a minor masterpiece that changed the face of horror films. It did not change the face of Simone Simon, however, and that was its secret. As Irena Dubrovna, a Yugoslavian dress designer, she suffers the curse of her race, but turns into a black panther off-screen. Lewton, a man of taste, abhorred the obvious. His belief was that it was not the thing seen but the thing unseen that truly frightened. This was terrifyingly translated into pictures by Jacques Tourneur, who had inherited no little of his father Maurice's pictorial talent. The taut, short, shadowy film worried Koerner, who had hoped for hairier stuff: but the $134,000 'B' finally brought in over four million dollars! Lewton was anything but pleased with his reward: a new title – *The Curse of the Cat People*! This sequel arrived in 1944, co-directed by Gunther Von Fritsch and Robert Wise. Simone Simon, killed as a panther, returns as a smiling ghost to aid and comfort her lonely little daughter. A brilliant piece of supernatural cinema, but a long way from horror.

I Walked With a Zombie (1943) was a long way, too, from those regular walking dead at the Monogram lot. The title was given Lewton by Koerner again, who had bought a series of articles by Inez Wallace, run under that heading in the Hearst

161

The Quickie and the Dead: Fast-buck flicks were churned out at top speed and the easiest-to-make monsters were zombies. The walking dead were easy to come by at the Hollywood extras' agencies. Height and eyeballs were all that was required from Darby Jones in *I Walked With a Zombie* (RKO 1943; *right*); the girls in *Voodoo Man* (Monogram 1944; *below right*) did not even need to have height. John Carradine had enough of that. Henry Victor was as wooden as his victims in *King of the Zombies* (Monogram 1941; *below left*). *Opposite:* George Zucco and Bela Lugosi put their heads together for *Voodoo Man* (Monogram 1944).

Sunday supplements. What Lewton gave Koerner back was 'Jane Eyre in the West Indies' (Lewton's phrase), even though Curt Siodmak wrote the screenplay. Tall Darby Jones played Carre Four, the zombie who towered over Frances Dee. She was the nurse who finds happiness with Tom Conway, a sugar planter whose wandering wife has been zombified by his mother. The title certainly didn't cheat the way *The Leopard Man* (1943) did. The third in a row from the Lewton-Tourneur team, it was mystery without horror or monsters, taken from Cornell Woolrich's thriller 'Black Alibi'. Mark Robson, who had edited all three, was now promoted to director and made *The Seventh Victim* (1943). This was also a debut for Kim Hunter as an orphan girl involved with Devil-worshippers in Greenwich Village. Robson's *The Ghost Ship* (1943) had no ghost, of course, unless it was that of Jack London who may have recognized his 'Sea Wolf' in Richard Dix.

Boris Karloff and Bela Lugosi now signed on at RKO. Koerner had suddenly died and the new man, Jack J. Gross, wanted a more traditional horror movie. *The Body Snatcher* (1945), a solo from Robert Wise, gave Karloff one of his finest roles. He played the grave Gray, cabman and specimen supplier to the medical trade. Robert Louis Stevenson's story of nineteenth-century Edinburgh provided a splendid role for neglected Henry Daniell (Dr MacFarlane) but a minor one for doomed Lugosi (Joseph). Everything built to a terrifying climax on a runaway coach. It went over the heads of the British audience: the censor cut it out.

Lugosi went over to RKO's other 'B' unit to put the wind up Brown and Carney in two frightening comedies, while Karloff stayed with Lewton for two very different frights, both with Mark Robson. *Isle of the Dead* (1945) continued Lewton's studio-built globe-trotting by setting itself off the coast of Greece. Karloff was General Nikolas Pherides, weakened by plague and bothered by vrykolakas, the local vampires. Banned in Britain for a while, the film was at least seen; more than can be said for *Bedlam* (1946), which the censor found beyond bearing. It was set in the infamous eighteenth-century institution for the insane, St Mary's of Bethlehem, inspired by William Hogarth's eighth painting in his series 'The Rake's Progress'. Karloff was Master George Sims, who put his patients to perform strange plays for the pleasure of the rich. This was the authentic horror of history, a use of the genre's star and style to illustrate truth. It was Karloff's last for Lewton and Lewton's last for RKO. He abandoned the 'B' hive

for 'A' features that were worth more in money but less in while. He died very suddenly in 1951. He was forty-six.

Universal, when they weren't making class 'A' horrors, made class 'B' ones instead. Sometimes as well! *The Mad Doctor of Market Street* (1941) was type-casting for Lionel Atwill. With him at the helm the audience knew what they were in for. Only the title cheated: one moment's madness in Market Street and Atwill spent the rest of the sixty minutes shipwrecked on a South Sea Island. There lay Princess Tanao, comatose. A swift jab with the old adrenalin and she is up and about, while natives fall on their knees and worship Atwill as their God of Life. Atwill returned in *The Strange Case of Dr RX* (1942). He played Dr Fish but was merely a red herring. The masked man determined to exchange the brain of his ape with that of Patric Knowles was none other than Samuel S. Hinds. Atwill lurked again in *The Night Monster* (1942), this time in company with Bela Lugosi. Both were red herrings in a *House of Mystery* (the British title) that demonstrated the power of mind over matter. Nils Asther's mind gave Ralph Morgan matter. This rich cripple grew new legs at will and

163

Females of the Species: Girls, more usually the done-to, as in *The Neanderthal Man* (Global 1953; *opposite left*), are occasionally the doers. A pioneer in the cause of Women's Lib was Nina Foch in *Cry of the Werewolf* (Columbia 1944; *below*). Her Queen Celeste of the Trioga Tribe was followed, duly if belatedly, by Deidre Biddulph (Ursula Howells) in *Dr Terror's House of Horrors* (Amicus 1964; *right*). Carol Thurston was the disfigured victim of a disfigured female who used *The Hypnotic Eye* (Allied Artists 1960; *opposite above right*), and Greek vrykolakas beset Ellen Drew in *Isle of the Dead* (RKO 1945; *opposite below right*).

thus wreaked surprising vengeance upon his more hidebound medical advisers. *The Mad Ghoul* (1943) was David Bruce, who took one whiff of George Zucco's gas and wrinkled alarmingly. Only a fresh heart would restore the youth to his cheeks and Evelyn Ankers to his arms.

The success of their *Mummy* saga inspired Universal to initiate an original 'B' movie monster series. The twist was, instead of the traditional plot of the monster and the girl, this time the monster *was* the girl: *Captive Wild Woman* (1943). John Carradine as Dr Sigmund Walters treated Cheela the orang-outang with glandular extractions from Martha MacVicar, and named the result Paula Dupree. But like the Panther Woman of America,

that stubborn old beast flesh comes creeping back. Under moments of emotional stress – she discovers Milburn Stone prefers the company of Evelyn Ankers – Paula goes ape. The gorilla girl saves her beloved from a circus stampede but is shot by mistake. Yet Acquanetta, who played her, was soon back in Jack Pierce's makeup as *Jungle Woman* (1944), revived from the dead by J. Carrol Naish, otherwise Dr Fletcher. He turned her into a girl again, but once more jealousy reared its, and Paula's, ugly head. Undaunted, Otto Kruger as Dr Stendhal set about reviving her corpse once more. In *Jungle Captive* (1944) Paula's changeover was indeed a change: the ape metamorphosed into Vicky Lane. Even this did not satisfy Kruger, how-

Atomic Boom: Outsize oddities bedevilled the world. In America there was *Tarantula* (Universal 1955; *opposite left*), *The Deadly Mantis* (Universal 1957; *opposite right*) and *The Black Scorpion* (Warner 1957; *left*). In Japan, which had known the other end of the atom, there was *Godzilla Versus the Thing* (Toho 1964; *opposite below*). The Thing was Mothra from the film of the same name. Then came *Space Amoeba* (1970; *bottom left*), *Gamera Versus Jiger* (1971; *bottom right*), and the celebratory monster party, *Destroy All Monsters* (1968; *below*).

changed to AIP – American International Pictures), and for the Corman formula. This was a sixty-minute running time, a ten-day shooting schedule, a minimal crew, an even more minimal cast (once he got it down to three!), a monster in a rubber suit, and a twist in the tail. Soon he was shooting his films in tandem, using the same sets, actors, crews: instant double bills. His casting was cut-price, fading 'B' players or young beginners, and this accidentally helped his horrors touch a new nerve. Corman's unknowns communicated with the teenagers in the drive-ins. AIP had tapped a new audience area. Young people liked Corman's throw-away movies and ultimately, ironically, made a cult hero of a director who was so cynical of the take-anything crowd that he even came to dispense with his monsters. *Beast With a Million Eyes* (1956) was an economically invisible force, while *Not Of This Earth* (1957) was Paul Birch in business suit and sunglasses! Except in the advertising; AIP were not that stupid. If anyone complained, Arkoff and Nicholson claimed their posters gave an 'artist's impression' of the films.

Nothing accelerates scientific progress like a war. In 1952 cinema itself went to war. The enemy: television. The secret weapon: a pair of spectacles. Arch Oboler, of all people, launched the attack. He was a man of words, a radio writer, creator of mental images of horror in 'Lights Out'. Now he whipped up an assault on the eyeballs called *Bwana Devil* (1952), which had as its slogan 'A Lion in your Lap!' Shot in polarized Natural Vision, it brought back the eye-blinking shock of George Barnes and his 1903 six-gun, with the added realism of three-dimensional Anscocolor. A cheap piece, it was not so much a spectacle, more a bespectacle, as audiences squinted behind obligatory glasses. More spectacular were its profits, and the big studios were quick to leap aboard the stereoscopical roller-coaster.

Warners, who had pioneered the sound wave, were first in the van of the new revolution. Once again Hollywood history repeated itself: the second 3-D movie was a horror film, and, of course, it was a remake. *House of Wax* (1953) was a full colour, full dimension rehash of *The Mystery of the Wax Museum*. The late Lionel Atwill's part went to velvet-toned Vincent Price, wearing a Warner-colorful new makeup by Gordon Bau. It re-established the star in the genre from which he had vanished long before, but the added dimension diminished the horror. Stereo separated the actors from the backgrounds but polished them into shimmery waxworks that worked in a rounded reality that was curiously unreal. The shocks came not from tangible horror but from a small ball, ping-ponged out of the screen directly at your nose.

André de Toth directed *House of Wax* with a surprising eye for 3-D detail. Even in polaroid specs de Toth saw everything 'flat'; he had only one eye. But as he pointed out, 'Beethoven couldn't hear music either, could he?' Roy Del Ruth, who had pioneered the dimension of sound with *The Terror*, now followed through in depth with *The Phantom of the Rue Morgue* (1954). This reworking of the Poe piece cast Karl Malden, a method man, as Dr Marais the Darwinian, but although he rolled his steroscopical eyeballs he was no Lugosi. Fox, busy with Cinemascope, let a subsidiary called Panoramic Productions try 3-D. They dusted off an old plot and an ape-suit and called it *Gorilla At Large* (1954). 'He's in the aisles! He's in the balcony! He's everywhere!' lied the posters, for inside the skin was a she, Anne Bancroft.

Robot Monster (1953) was the first science-fiction film in stereo, but whilst the hairy Ro-Man blew 3-D bubbles, the monsters remained stubbornly 2-D: they were stock shots from *One Million BC*! The same producer, Al Zimbalist, sent Sonny Tufts into space to confront *Cat-Women of the Moon* (1954), a telepathic tribe played by the stereoscopic 'Hollywood Cover Girls'. The surprise of both movies comes only in retrospect: their music was written by Elmer Bernstein.

Universal, home of horror, took naturally to Natural Vision, but where Warners had looked back to vintage monsters, the old firm took an unexpected look into the future. Combining the trend towards science-fiction with the fashionable fad for location filming, Jack Arnold directed *It*

Space Race: The inhuman race from outer space ranged from the tentacled head of the *Invaders From Mars* (Twentieth Century-Fox 1953; *opposite*) to Ray 'Crash' Corrigan in a baggy suit as *It! The Terror From Beyond Space* (UA 1958; *right*). Somewhere between comes the po-faced big-head *The Man From Planet X* (UA 1951; *below left*) and his muscle-bound contemporary *Phantom From Space* (UA 1953; *below right*).

Swinging Poe: Edgar Allan Poe has proved inspirational to the American horror movie from the days of D. W. Griffith. Unhappily, the master poet of the macabre mood does not transpose well to the cinema screen, beyond the mere illustration of his classic devices. *The Pit and the Pendulum*, first filmed in the silent period, popped up in *The Raven* (Universal 1935; *right*), which was more Boris and Bela than Edgar Allan. Roger Corman filmed it with Vincent Price in 1961, then sent it, him, and themselves up in *Dr Goldfoot and the Bikini Machine* (American International 1965; *below*).

Came From Outer Space (1953). Ray Bradbury's story of wandering Xenomorphs, aliens of misty aspect, was futuristic stuff, yet behind it the old horrors lurked. The small town in the Arizona desert stood in for the cut-off community of European yore; the glamour-gowned girl, possessed in mind in the wind-blown night, was a bride of Dracula; the stolid citizens, mindless zombies in the dark, were somnambulists straight from Caligari's Cabinet.

Universal and Arnold manufactured a brand new monster specifically for stereo. The Gill-Man was an Amazonian throw-back, but he acted pretty much like the old monsters. *Creature From the Black Lagoon* (1954) was Ben Chapman, a swimmer in a rubber suit that made him a literal frogman. Designers Bud Westmore and Jack Kevan gave him a fierce fish-face, fins and flippers, but no visible reason for abducting swimsuited Julia Adams. The underwater sequences stood out in an otherwise damp entry. But the box office warranted a return, and there duly came *Revenge of the Creature* (1955), which brought the Gill-Man to Florida. Neither Arnold, Chapman, nor the third dimension were involved in the last of the series, *The Creature Walks Among Us* (1956). Ricou Browning was the Gill-Man until Dr Jeff Morrow operated upon him; then he became Don Megowan. The sinuous swimmer, elegant in his own element, turns into a shambling, clumsy hulk, pathetic as he harks to the strange call of the oceans, ugly in his sackcloth Frankenstein suit. For once, man is the monster, the monster his victim. Last seen the Gill-Man was heading out to sea, preserving sufficient natural instinct to steer clear of Abbott and Costello.

The men who made the decision to drop the Bomb have much to answer for, in life and in movies. The fall-out was far-flung. The Atomic Age began, for Hollywood, eight years after Hiroshima. The Army is A-testing in the Arctic.

'Every time we let one off I feel like I'm writing the first chapter of the new Genesis.'
'Let's hope we're not writing the last chapter of the old!'

The conscience is ignored, the button is pressed, and the fury let loose upon the world. But this time it takes physical form in the prehistoric person of a rhedosaur, aroused from its hundred-million-year deepfreeze. *The Beast From 20,000 Fathoms* (1953) burst an iceberg, crashed down Coney Island, and bowled over the box office. It set a behaviour pattern for countless followers: re-awakened creatures, magnified monstrosities, intergalactic invaders. An atomic test, an initial sighting ignored, a climactical rampage, and an ultimate extinction by radioactive weaponry, a variation of the force that gave the menace life.

Although the Beast is credited to a Ray Bradbury tale, 'The Fog Horn', its true parent is undoubtedly the dinosaur that destroyed London in Willis O'Brien's original *Lost World*. Ray Harryhausen, O'Brien's youthful disciple (he reckons to have seen *King Kong* more times than its animator), built and operated the Beast, which at 25,000 dollars was the main item on the movie's 180,000 dollar budget. The producers were two old Monogram men: Jack Dietz, who with Sam Katzman had run the East Side Kids series, and Hal E. Chester, who had been one of those very Kids. Chester it was who, producing *Night of the Demon* (1958) in England, insisted on showing the materialized monster. Critics complained, but Chester knew the box-office potential of full-frontal crudity.

Ray Harryhausen took up where O'Brien left off and did it all again with an octopus in *It Came From Beneath the Sea* (1955), extra-terrestrials in *Earth Versus the Flying Saucers* (1956), and an Ymir from Venus in *Twenty Million Miles to Earth* (1957). Along with his producer, Charles Schneer, Harryhausen switched to fantasy. He shot the first Technicolor confrontation between man and model monster in *The Seventh Voyage of Sinbad* (1957). His system, a unique mixture of earlier methods, is called Dynamation (when it isn't called Superdynamation).

A second side-effect of the nuclear explosion was enlargement. *Them!* (1953) were ants, atomically expanded to fifteen-foot lengths, who came jingling out of the New Mexico desert with lethal injections of formic acid at the ready. *Monster From the Ocean Floor* (1954) was a magnified protozoon; *It Came From Beneath the Sea* (1955) an outsize octopus; *The Phantom From 10,000 Leagues* (1955) a marine mutation; *Monster From Green Hell* (1956) a thirty-foot queen wasp; and *Monster That Challenged the World* (1957) a colossal caterpillar. Self-explanatory were *Tarantula* (1955), *Attack of the Crab Monsters* (1957), *The Deadly Mantis* (1957), *The Giant Claw* (1957), *The Black Scorpion* (1957), *The Spider* (1958), *The Killer Shrews* (1959), *The Giant Gila Monster* (1959), and *Attack of the Giant Leeches* (1959). The monsters were proportionate to their budgets, not so much in size as in concept. If Harryhausen animated his magnified

Insanity Claws: The old 'Clutching Hand' of silent serial days still grabs them where it counts. Ann Robinson is tapped on the shoulder by a Martian in *The War of the Worlds* (Paramount 1953; *above left*), and Yvette Mimieux meets a Morlock in *The Time Machine* (MGM 1960; *above right*). *The Return of the Fly* (Twentieth Century-Fox 1959) came as a surprise to Danielle De Metz (*right*), as did the emergent *Gorgo* (King 1960; *opposite*) to two torchlight fishermen.

178

monsters, chances were the film would be good. At the other end of the scale was Bert I. Gordon and his back-projected insects.

Bert Gordon was the man who, when Universal and Jack Arnold reversed the expanding trend with *The Incredible Shrinking Man* (1957), an atomic variation of Browning's old *Devil Doll*, came up with a reversed reverse: *The Amazing Colossal Man* (1957). Glenn Langan played a bald colonel who grew ten feet a day, thanks to the power of a plutonium explosion and a back-projection screen. The army mowed him down on the Boulder Dam, yet he returned a year later for *War of the Colossal Beast* (1958). Still seventy feet tall and bald, he looked slightly different: he had a hole in his head and was played by Dean Parkin. When a rival producer nipped in with *Attack of the Fifty Foot Woman* (1958), Gordon was undaunted. Remembering the Universal picture that had inspired it all, Gordon struck back with *Attack of the Puppet People* (1958), which was released in England as *Six Inches Tall*.

Meanwhile your common or garden dinosaur was undergoing a revival of interest, and nuclear tests were often the cause of its revival, too. Willis O'Brien was behind *The Beast of Hollow Mountain* (1956), the first monster movie made both in Regiscope and Mexico. O'Brien and Eugene Lourie,

who had directed *The Beast From 20,000 Fathoms*, came to London on location to knock down the docks for *The Giant Behemoth* (1959), and Lourie did it again on his own with *Gorgo* (1960). O'Brien returned home for *The Lost World* (1960) in colour (this time he used live monsters – reptiles in costume), but his influence remained: *Konga* (1961) was a British piece about, of course, an outsize ape. O'Brien died in 1962. Seven years later his protégé Ray Harryhausen completed a prehistoric piece O'Brien had begun for RKO back in 1942. *The Valley of Gwangi* (1969) had its dynamated dinosaur burn to death in a Spanish cathedral, but no room in its credits for O'Brien.

O'Brien's Kong remains the giant of them all, the fifty-foot yardstick against which all monsters are measured. Even *Godzilla, King of the Monsters* (1955) was billed as 'Makes King Kong look like a Midget!' – but only in actual inches. This 400-foot dragon who took on Tokyo (Tokyo lost!) was but an actor in creature's clothing compared to the animated ape. He stomped around a model city, breathing fire and fury, pushing down skyscrapers, chomping up railway trains, tromping on ocean liners, laughing off the mere tickle of high-voltage shocks. Big spectacle but on a miniature scale, engineered in the painstaking tradition of the

Head for the Hills! Scarcely a city was left standing under the onslaught of outsize monsters during the Atomic Age of Cinema. New York was knocked down by *The Beast From 20,000 Fathoms* (Warner 1953; *opposite top left*), Stockholm by *Reptilicus* (Cinemagic 1962; *opposite top right*), Tokyo by *Godzilla, King of the Monsters* (Toho 1954; *left and opposite below*) and again by *King Kong Versus Godzilla* (Toho 1962; *below left*), and London by *Gorgo* (King 1960; *below*).

181

Fish School: The underwater world still holds a few surprises. Lionel Barrymore discovered a whole race of fishmen as far back as 1929: *The Mysterious Island* (MGM; *right*). Julia Adams discovered the prehistoric Gill-Man up the Amazon and got carried away: *Creature From the Black Lagoon* (Universal 1954; *below left*). Miss Adams and he were in 3-D. Ricou Browning swam the part again in *Revenge of the Creature* (Universal 1955; *opposite*) but after his operation Don Megowan took the part: *The Creature Walks Among Us* (Universal 1956; *below right*). A later Gill-Man appeared briefly in *City Under the Sea* (page 169), known in America as *War-Gods of the Deep*.

Japanese craftsman by Eiji Tsuburuya.

Gojira was Japan's first international success. Directed by Inoshiro Honda in 1954, the Toho company sold it to America where new scenes were inserted by Terry Morse, with Raymond Burr as reporter Steve Martin. He finds Tokyo in the same kind of panic that had gripped New York the year before when attacked by that Beast from 20,000 Fathoms. The Bikini Bomb has awakened a monster who is on the loose. Being a Japanese monster, Godzilla is mythic. He breathes fire like all true dragons, but with a modern touch: Godzilla's fire is radioactive. Ancient islanders have been appeasing their local legend, Kong-like, with the annual gift of a girl on a raft. Scientists now send Godzilla a depth-bomb instead. In return the outraged dragon razes Tokyo and is finally killed when a Dr Seriza destroys all the oxygen in the sea. The awful responsibility of this deadly decision makes the doctor commit hara-kiri.

Godzilla, an atomic allegory created by the victims to shock the conscience of the victors, backfired. It was a victory for commercialization over contamination, and despite his definitive death Godzilla came roaring back. There was *Godzilla's Counterattack* (1955), *Godzilla Versus the Thing* (1964), *Son of Godzilla* (1966), *Godzilla Versus Hedorah* (1971), and even *King Kong Versus Godzilla* (1962). O'Brien's old ape proved truly immortal: Honda and Tsuburaya revived him yet again in *King Kong Escapes* (1967). Godzilla also turned up in *Ebirah, Horror of the Deep* (1966). This time on 'our' side, he saved the world from an incredible crab.

Godzilla was one of the many 'guest stars' in *Destroy All Monsters* (1968), Toho's celebratory twentieth monster movie rally. Most of the Japanese creatures came, a role which by now includes *Half-Human* (1955), an abominable snowman; *Rodan* (1956), a terrible pterodactyl; *Varan the Unbelievable* (1961), a scaly prehistoric beast; *Mothra* (1961), a monster moth; *Gorath* (1962), a prehistoric reptile; *Matanga, Fungus of Terror* (1963); *Dogora the Space Monster* (1964), a giant

Same Name: *Frankenstein 1970* (Allied Artists 1958; *below*) and *Frankenstein Conquers the World* (Toho 1965; *right*) are but two of the modern-made horror films to cash-in on the non-cop title. Universal's monster makeup remains in copyright, however, which makes other studios' monsters but pale imitations. Other name-droppers include *Frankenstein Meets the Space Monster* and *Jesse James Meets Frankenstein's Daughter*.

BORIS KARLOFF
in
"FRANKENSTEIN-1970" "X"
CinemaScope
AN ALLIED ARTISTS PICTURE
DISTRIBUTED BY ASSOCIATED BRITISH-PATHE

jellyfish; *Ghidrah the Three-Headed Monster* (1964), a three-headed monster; *Gamera* (1965), a turtle with teeth; *Majin* (1966), a walking statue; *Ebirah, Horror of the Deep* (1966), a colossal crab; *Gappa the Triphibian Monster* (1967), a beaky lizard; *The X From Outer Space* (1967), an X from outer space; *Gyaos* (1967), a fanged and flying fox; *Viras* (1967), a squid from space; *Goke, Bodysnatcher From Hell* (1968), a vampire jelly; *Jiger* (1969); *Space Amoeba* (1970), and *Zigra* (1971). Every year Tokyo, Yokohama, Osaka and points east are razed to the ground; every year the monsters are destroyed; and every year Tokyo and Co rise again, as do the monsters. It is a circle of cinematic spectacle that shows no sign of disappearing up its own sprockethole. As long as it continues, vicariously satisfying a human urge to destroy, it may keep real-life destruction at bay.

Radioactive contamination mutated the traditional horror film, too. Poor old Bela Lugosi was the first to suffer. In *Bride of the Atom* (1955) he tried to make an atomic superman but what he got was Tor Johnson, a bald and bulgy wrestler. Zombies got the nuclear treatment in *Creature With the Atom Brain* (1955), a Curt Siodmak script. Steven Ritch turned into *The Werewolf* (1956), victim of a misguided plan for H-Bomb survival, and John Beal was the atomic scientist who drew blood as *The Vampire* (1957). Boris Karloff, too, suffered from fall-out. He played Baron Victor, last of the Frankensteins (and Karloff's first as a genuine member of the family) in *Frankenstein 1970*, which was made in 1958. He used an atomic reactor to revive his ancestor's experiment; they both perished in a gush of 'atomic steam'.

> 'Children of all ages should be allowed to see horror films. I am sure that Frankenstein and Dracula would not have any serious effect on children's minds. After all, I saw them myself when I was a kid, and they didn't affect me!'

Herman Cohen, producer, protesting against the British censor's decision to award his film an 'X' for Adults Only certificate, and failing to give credit where it was due. For without his own early exposure to Karloff and Lugosi, would he have created one of the greatest titles in the history of movies, *I Was A Teenage Werewolf* (1957)? It deserved its stupendous success at the box office: Cohen's investment of 150,000 dollars profited him nearly two-and-a-half million. He almost did it again with *I Was a Teenage Frankenstein* (1957),

but none of his instant imitators came anywhere near, even with *Teenage Monster* (1957), *Teenage Zombies* (1958), *Teenage Cavemen* (1958), or *Teenagers From Outer Space* (1959). Cohen came to England to make *I Was a Teenage Gorilla*, but by the time it was ready there had been too many teenagers on the scene for even as keen a teenlover as Cohen. The film went out as *Konga* (1961).

In the changing pattern of picture-making, the independent producer has emerged to replace the old 'B' picture units run by the major studios. William Castle, like Charles Schneer and Herman Cohen, has a fondness for the fantastic, and also like the others shuttles between America and England. Unlike them, however, Castle also directs his own films. He learned his quick trade turning out *Boston Blackie*, *Whistler*, and *Crime Doctor* series in Columbia's 'B' unit, but is economically unable to give his independent productions that built-in big studio gloss. He makes up for this by wildly imaginative devices to pull in his public.

Macabre (1955) began it all: the audience was issued with thousand-dollar insurance policies against being scared to death. Castle played it safe: the movie was little more than a murder mystery. 'Emergo' was the gimmick with *The House on Haunted Hill* (1958): as Vincent Price turns a handle on screen, a dangling skeleton cranks across the auditorium (provided the projectionist is on cue!). Price was back in *The Tingler* (1959), warning the audience that materialized fright in the shape of a clutching crab was loose among them. Lucky patrons felt its touch when their electrically-wired seats gave them a shock! 'Ghost Viewers' were handed out with the tickets for *13 Ghosts* (1960), red/green glasses that added an extra dimension to the materializations. Cohen followed Castle by inserting 'Hypnovista' sequences into the American release print of his British *Horrors of the Black Museum* (1959), but the craze for Psychoramas, Fright Breaks, and stereo 'Masks' seems to have gone the way of 3-D. Castle's most frightening film to date has been the only one he did not direct: Roman Polanski's *Rosemary's Baby* (1968).

The macabre melancholy of Edgar Allan Poe had attracted American movie-makers for fifty years. The lure of Poe's poetics may have been the desire to create a genuinely native horror film, the challenge to translate his imaginative imagery into movie visuals, or the fact that he was out of copyright. To 1960 the most successful movies, as

The Corman Cometh: Roger Corman, whizz-kid of the quickies, came to England to make *Masque of the Red Death* (American International 1964). He might as well have stayed at home, for the end-product was just like his other pieces of Poe, right down to his star, Vincent Price. British budgeting did allow for a few more extras to be available for the orgy scene, however (*right*). Hazel Court's sacrificial slashing (*below*) was cut by the British Censor. *Opposite:* John Beal as *The Vampire* (Gramercy 1957) keeps the home fires burning.

186

Price of Fame: Vincent Price is today's king of the horror movie, the inheritor of Karloff's crown. Seldom a man for monstrous makeup, Price permutates his familiar features with a trimming of whiskers, a brush of pomade, a pair of dark glasses. *Opposite* he is seen in *The Tomb of Ligeia* (American International 1964; *above*), yet another pot of Poe by Corman, and *below*, surrounded by the mutants of *The Haunted Palace* (American International 1963). This was pretended Poe by Corman. *Above left*, Price is in Poe-Corman's *House of Usher* (American International 1960), and, *left*, in Corman-Poe's *The Raven* (American International 1963). Peeping round is Peter Lorre. *Above* is the Price poster for *House on Haunted Hill* (Allied Artists 1958), by William Castle for a change.

horror movies, had been the Universal series, which had simply taken a Poe title and theme and let Karloff and Lugosi take it from there. Suddenly Poe found a new interpreter in, of all people, Roger Corman. The king of the quickies was tired of making back-to-back movies. Now, he asked American International, instead of making two pictures for the price of one, could he make one for the price of two? Nicholson and Arkoff, aghast, were aghast again when Corman told them the tale he had in mind was 'The Fall of the House of Usher'. Acutely aware of their teenage audience, one half of AIP pointed out that as high school students had to study Poe they would naturally hate him! The other half pointed out that there was no monster in the story, and horror pictures had to have a monster. 'The house is the monster,' retorted glib Mr Corman.

House of Usher (1960) had everything that Corman's quickies lacked. Colour (Pathecolor applied with unusual selectivity), CinemaScope (photographed with unusual mobility by Floyd Crosby), music (written with unusual sensitivity by Les Baxter), mood (designed with unusual period sense by Daniel Haller), literacy (scripted with unusual care by novelist Richard Matheson), acting (played with unusual restraint by Vincent Price). Unfortunately it also had length, eighty minutes compared with the usual sixty, and the extra twenty minutes made their presence felt early on as it became clear that Corman had not been able to avoid one hangover from his old days: a low budget. Having paid for his big star he had room for only three more actors. As two of these were in the teenage mould, insurance for AIP's

regular customers, the longueurs were longer than ever. In a desperate bid for variety Corman threw in a shot in which the entire Usher family tree materialized in the form of ten bit-part players. Yet riding as it did upon the Hammer wave of horror, the fall of Usher marked the rise of Corman.

Suddenly, it's Poe! Having run his monsters, teenagers, rock'n'rollers, and dragstrippers into the ground, Corman embarked upon a cinematic campaign to do the same for poor Poe. *The Pit and the Pendulum* (1961); *The Premature Burial* (1962); *Tales of Terror* (1962) which were 'The Case of M. Valdemar', 'The Black Cat', and 'Morella'; *The Raven* (1963); *The Haunted Palace* (1963), which was really H.P.Lovecraft's 'The Case of Charles Dexter Ward'; *The Masque of the Red Death* (1964); *The Tomb of Ligeia* (1964). The last two Corman made in England, yet hardly needed to have made the trip. They were as much formula as the others; the dominant Price, the arty credits, the tracking shots, the familiar corridors, the old house.

Even with his luxurious new schedules, four weeks instead of two, Corman felt the urge to rush things. *The Raven* was polished off with three days to spare. Instead of giving his star, the venerable Boris Karloff, a breather, Corman had a script whipped up overnight, and while two assistants shot backgrounds in the Big Sur, he propped his aged trouper against those *Raven* sets still standing and called the hastily-pasted end-product *The Terror* (1963).

The difference between the formula-bound Corman and a film-maker can be seen in the work of one of his protégés, Peter Bogdanovich. Using Corman techniques – clips from *The Terror* spliced into improvised location shooting, plus two days of Boris Karloff's services left over from a Corman contract – Bagdanovich made *Targets* (1968). It was a brilliant debut by any standards, and remains one of Karloff's finest films ever. The grand old monster plays himself, thinly disguised as Byron Orlok, musing over the golden age of horror films, disliking modern trends in the genre, then accidentally caught up in real-life horror involving a teenage sniper. Karloff made more films before he died in England, on 2 February 1969, at the age of eighty-two. But it is *Targets* that remains, the perfect obituary, and the only horror film completely to bridge the gap between the horror that was golden and the horror that is today.

Unwelcome Visitors: *Invisible Invaders* (UA 1959; *above*); *Willard* (Crosby 1970; *opposite*).

THE BEST OF BRITISH BLOOD

In which there is a Murder at the Red Barn, a Face at the Window, a Demon Barber in Fleet Street, and blood on the Hammer.

The Frankenstein Monster, Dr Jekyll and Mr Hyde, Count Dracula, The Invisible Man: in order of their appearance, the great monsters of literature. And all British. Karloff, Clive, Laughton, Thesiger, Rains, Rathbone, Atwill, Banks, Hardwicke, Zucco: the great players of horror, as British as R.C.Sherriff who wrote and James Whale who directed. A heritage of horror, hallowed by Hollywood, ignored by England.

The horror film was the perfect native product: yet it was untouched by an industry that sneered at America's England, that fogbound London of hansom cabbies and bribable bobbies, equalled only by fogbound Cornwall or fogbound Wales, where the autumn moon beamed, the wolfbane bloomed, the garlic wreathed, and there was breathing in the barn. Universal Europe: where the moors of Llanwelly subbed for the plains of Vasaria, where villagers crossed themselves in cockney or 'country' before lighting their flaming torches and proceeding up the Borgo Pass. The settings were interchangeable, the ambiance unchangeable. This was the secret of the Universal universe. It gave the great films a continuity that was comforting to come back to, whatever the horror that walked abroad. Familiar faces, familiar places: a sort of security in a world of fear. It was easier to suspend belief when the impossible took place in a tight, false world of studio-built landscape, where every tree was carefully gnarled in expressionistic fright, every house cunningly gabled in Gothic mystery, every shadow beautifully lit into lurking terror; and where every actor was caught in the closing ring of horrors, untouched by the possibility of a normal world beyond. Perhaps, then, it was for the best that British cinema left the horrors to Hollywood.

One other great British tradition almost made it as a native school of horror movie: the theatre of blood and thunder. The Victorian taste for vicarious violence was satisfied by the once-weekly, twice-nightly welter of gore called melodrama.

William Corder had murdered Maria Marten, mistress and mole-catcher's daughter, in 1827. Her old mother dreamed the body was in the barn. The floor was dug up, the corpse uncovered, and Corder was hanged. The case and its supernatural solution caught the public's fancy. It was re-enacted by puppets and peep-shows, penny dreadfuls and penny-gaffs, and remained in repertory for more than a century. Dicky Winslow, a theatrical gent who stage-managed the movies sold by George Harrison & Co of Berners Street (today we would call him the director), cranked his camera on a sketch company version then touring the Music Halls. *Maria Martin; or, The Murder in the Red Barn* (1902) packed six scenes into five minutes: Maria's Disguise . . . The Murder in the Red Barn . . . The Dream . . . The Arrest of Corder . . . The Condemned Cell . . . The Apparition of Maria. Mr and Mrs A.W.Fitzgerald played Corder and Maria, then immediately played the leads in an unlikely item called *A Fight With Sledgehammers* (1902).

Melodrama went West: to Wales where William Haggar toured the village fairgrounds as 'The Old'un of Aberdare'. One of his sideshows was the Great American Bioscope and he used it to turn out his own flickering epics. With his enormous family playing all the parts, Haggar's Sensationals were snapped up by the London offices of Frenchman Gaumont and American Urban. Their main English trade was with the fairground exhibitors and Haggar knew exactly what those wanderers, and their audiences, wanted. Where Harrison produced complete, if condensed, stories, Haggar showed simply the meat. And red meat it was.

The Two Orphans (1902), Adolphe Dennery's mighty melodrama, came out as 'A knife duel between a Cripple and a Marquis'. *True as Steel* (1902), 'scenes from the drama of the same name', was little more than a 'Sensational fight between

Bars Sinister: Boris Karloff as *The Ghoul* (Gaumont British 1933).

a Knight and a Forest Hermit'. Of Haggar's remaining releases for 1902 apparently titles alone were enough to guarantee sales: *The Wild Man of Borneo* and *The Maniac's Guillotine*. Haggar caught wind of *The Life of Charles Peace* (1905) being filmed in Sheffield, and rushed through his own version, casting son Walter as 'The Modern Ishmael'. Haggar's grisly climax, a realistic representation of the murderous burglar's execution, must have stirred memories for the older generation: Haggar's movie was the first public hanging since 1868! The Sheffield Photo Company was more squeamish: 'It has been decided *not* to reproduce the Execution Scene, as we believe it is too ghastly and repulsive.' Haggar got round to Corder's crime, too, but evidently the confusion of the two Charley Peace films left their mark. Haggar reversed his title to *The Red Barn Crime; or, Maria Martin* (1908). Son Walter, as Corder, was hanged again. Maurice Elvey, who would finally emerge as Britain's most prolific popular director, was the first to get the girl's name right. His *Maria Marten; or, The Murder in the Red Barn* (1913) was even more historic. Elvey actually filmed it in the original Red Barn in Polstead, Suffolk. Fred Groves was the squire and Elizabeth Risdon the farmer's daughter.

That last year of peace saw a small revival in British films and British horror. *Dr Trimball's Verdict* (1913), a Cecil Hepworth Production, had Alec Worcester as the doctor who murders his rival. Later he buys a skeleton for his study. It turns out to be his victim's: his ghost materializes upon his own bones. Dr Trimball dies of shock. *The Vampire* (1913) was set in India and showed a native lady turning into a snake to bite the explorer who shot her. *The Grip of Iron* (1913), Arthur Shirley's melodrama founded upon 'Les Etrangleurs de Paris', was filmed in Brighton. Fred Powell played the insurance clerk who secretly strangled for the sake of his extravagant daughter. *The Fakir's Spell* (1914) changed an Indian girl's English lover into a gorilla. He is captured by a circus, but reverts to his old self when his cage catches fire. *Heba the Snake Woman* (1915) was a transformation too: identical with *The Vampire* except Heba was an Aztec. *A Cry in the Night* (1915) was heard when the heroine's father was killed by a mad doctor's winged gorilla. Under the fur and feathers was James Russell, an ex-Karno comic.

The first feature-length British horror was *The Avenging Hand* (1915): the ghost of an Egyptian Princess came to London looking for her severed member. There was a hypnotized chimp that strangled to order in *Crime and the Penalty* (1916), and *The Man Without a Soul* (1916) was Milton Rosmer back from the dead. George Loane Tucker directed this rather religious piece, then went home to America to make *The Miracle Man*. Leal Douglas was another spectral emigrant from Ancient Egypt. She brought vengeance upon an MP in – and as – *The Beetle* (1919). The strangler of Paris struck again in *The Grip of Iron* (1920); this time the doubled-up Jagon and Simmonnet was played by George Foley. Paris was again the setting for a film of an 1897 melodrama by F. Brooke Warren, whose title gave the world a phrase of fright.

The Face at the Window (1920), with its science-fictional set-piece of a corpse revived by electricity, also had the double-life ploy. Banker Lucio Degradoff is even less innocent than he sounds. By night he is Le Loup (The Wolf), a murdering burglar. His latest victim was killed in the act of writing: 'I am murdered by Luc. . . .' Naturally, handsome bank-clerk Lucien Cartwright is arrested, but an application of galvanism by Dr LeBlanc enables the corpse to complete his final act. He writes '. . . io' and the right man is copped by detective C. Aubrey Smith.

Grand Guignol arrived in England in 1921 in a series of short films of that generic title. Tales filmed included George Saxon's *A Bit of Black Stuff* and G.B.Stern's *The Curse of Westacott*. It was a time for shorts, and Lyn Harding played Svengali in a potted *Trilby* (1922) while Booth Conway was Quasimodo to Sybil Thorndike's *Esmeralda* (1922). A short story blown to feature length was W.W.Jacobs' classic *The Monkey's Paw* (1923): Moore Marriott and Marie Ault wished their dead son alive again and quickly wished they hadn't.

Adrian Brunel, who had played the lively corpse in *The Face at the Window*, promoted himself to director for *The Man Without Desire* (1923). There was a sensation at the première when a woman screamed and fainted as Ivor Novello clambered out of his coffin. A foretaste of different screams to come for England's greatest matinée idol. In the film he was Count Vittorio Dondolo who, distraught when his sweetheart is poisoned, submits to a scientist's experiment in suspended animation. Revived 300 years later he encounters his old love's descendant but alas, the old spark has gone.

Dead Heads: Decapitation has increased in popularity since Claude Rains was *The Man Who Reclaimed His Head* in 1934. Peter Lorre lost his head in *Tales of Terror* (1962), a typical Price-Poe-Corman-American International picture (*below*). *Right:* one of *The Four Skulls of Jonathan Drake* (Vogue 1959) as shrunk by Paul Wexler. *Bottom left: The Man Without a Body* (Eros 1957) was Nostradamus. *Bottom right: The Curse of the Living Corpse* (Twentieth Century-Fox 1964).

Faces at the Window: *opposite, Vampyr* (Dreyer 1932; *above left*) and *The Ghost Breakers* (Paramount 1940; *above right*); *below, Curse of the Dead* (F.U.L. 1966).

Familiar Faces: If the face isn't familiar, the makeup is. British horror films tend to go for American stars like Akim Tamiroff (*opposite above left*), who got atomically mixed with *The Vulture* (Paramount 1966), Bryant Haliday who was anatomically mixed as *The Projected Man* (Compton 1966; *opposite above right*) and Joan Crawford who got mixed up with *Trog* (Cohen 1970; *opposite below*). Boris Karloff, American star born in Britain, came home for *Grip of the Strangler* (MGM 1958; *left*) and Herman Cohen, American producer, came over for *Horrors of the Black Museum* (1959; *below*). Hammer, usually derivative, tried a new tack by turning Jacqueline Pearce into *The Reptile* (1966; *below left*).

199

Dr Fu Manchu looked anything but a Yellow Peril in the person of Harry Agar Lyons, but Harry Rignold was ideally cast as *The Coughing Horror* (1924). This hirsute henchman, flogged into fury, climbed through Nayland Smith's window and got his arm chopped off for his pains.

British films experienced a revival in the late silent period, thanks to the Government's new Quota Act. *Maria Marten* (1928) was revived, too, with Warwick Ward and Trilby Clark. Walter West directed, as he did a companion piece, *Sweeney Todd* (1928). Moore Marriott played the Demon Barber of Fleet Street, first seen in 1847 in the melodrama, 'The String of Pearls', by George Dibdin Pitt. This legend of bloody butchery – the barber uses his cut-throat razor to slash his customers and tip them into his cellar, whence the corpses are cooked into penny pies by the lady next door – turned out, in this version, to be a dream. The last silent movie in the genre was *Chamber of Horrors* (1929): Frank Stanmore going mad whilst spending the night in Madame Tussaud's waxworks. Again, it was all a dream.

The first true horror films arrived in Britain in 1931, and nobody was more horrified than the British censor. He cut them, fussed in the press, and initiated a system of 'Notification to the Home Office' for films 'of an horrific nature'. If any British studio had wanted to make horror films, this was more than enough to put them off. British films were carefully budgeted to bring returns on full circuit distribution: a limitation of patrons to the over-sixteens would completely eliminate profits. Only the smallest, cheapest studio dared to flirt with the form. *Castle Sinister* (1932) was made by Delta at Bushey. Eric Adeney failed to insert the

British Tradition: The traditional British melodrama could have found its film form with Tod Slaughter, who near-burlesqued himself in *Crimes At the Dark House* (King 1940; *above*). Earlier, Harry Rignold played a silent *Coughing Horror* (Stoll 1924; *above left*); later Karloff played *The Man Who Changed His Mind* (Gaumont 1936; *opposite*).

heroine's brain into an apeman's head, just as Widgey Newman failed to direct a good film. He failed again with *The Unholy Quest* (1934), despite letting R.W.Lotinga direct. Claude Bailey failed to revive an embalmed crusader. More successful was Leslie Hiscott's remake of *The Face at the Window* (1932). This time Raymond Massey sorted out Lucio Fournal from Lucien Courtier via Dr Renard's machinery.

Boris Karloff came home in 1933. It was a working holiday. He called on his delighted brothers, then made *The Ghoul* (1933) at Shepherd's Bush. It was old home week on all counts, for as Professor Morlant, Egyptologist, he rose glowing from his grave to seek a sacred jewel. Cedric Hardwicke lent stolid support and Ernest Thesiger lent his nostrils. T. Hayes Hunter's piece of fogbound Gothic, photographed by Gunther Krampf, was the only British horror film in the true Hollywood tradition, and the first to be 'notified as horrific'. This honour was also awarded to two more minor works, Brian Desmond Hurst's *The Tell-Tale Heart* (1934) from Poe, and Vernon Sewell's *The Medium* (1934). Sewell used his ghostly inspiration, a *Grand Guignol* play called 'L'Angoisse', four or more times during his directorial career.

Karloff came back for *The Man Who Changed His Mind* (1936), a clever title suiting John Balderston's story of personality exchange, dropped by the Americans for the more box-office *The Man Who Lived Again*. Karloff was Dr Laurience, swapping magnate Frank Cellier's

New Blood: Hammer tapped a new vein of horror when they turned on the Technicolor: blood ran red and is still running. Poe's *The Black Cat* (*right*) was given the new look by Hemisphere Pictures in 1966, while, *below left*, Edith Scob wears a mask to conceal her flayed flesh in *Eyes Without a Face* (Champs-Elysées 1960). Georges Franju's clinical experiment was shown in America as *Horror Chamber of Dr Faustus*. Tissue transplants also upset Alberto Lupo in *Seddok* (Lion 1960; *below right*). Another Italian monster was Doctor Hichcock, who first had an *Orribile Segreto*, then struck back as *The Spectre* (Panda 1963; *opposite above left*). *The Blood Beast Terror* (Tigon 1967; *opposite above right*) was an outsize death's-head moth. *Opposite below:* the chlorophyll man, a Philippino favourite, was all washed up in *Mad Doctor of Blood Island* (Hemisphere 1970) – but struck again in *Blood Devils*.

It sparked off cycles, spun off sequels, inspired revivals. 'This is where we came in'; but this time there was a difference. The new age of horror was geared to a new taste. Where the old films had quickly cut away from the sight of blood, Hammer cut in for a closeup. The old age had been a golden one in spite of its monochrome. The new age would be red, red as blood, and all in Glorious but inexpensive Eastmancolor.

Christopher Lee's Monster had little of Karloff's pathos, none of Karloff's appearance. The novel was out of copyright; not so Universal's movie. Phil Leakey plastered up the new 'Creature' (even its name was changed, just to be safe) and mid-way through the movie shot half its face away. Hammer made one fatal error: they killed the Creature in an acid bath. So when the time came for a sequel, they made Frankenstein the continuing thread instead. Peter Cushing played the Baron four more times, each time making a different Monster. Finally, running out of ideas, Hammer went back to the beginning again and remade their first film. *Horror of Frankenstein* (1970) introduced Ralph Bates as the more modern Prometheus.

Lee was promoted to *Dracula* (1958), a film which, like that vampire, had difficulty in crossing running water. Universal's copyright meant it had to be shown in America as *Horror of Dracula*. Reduced to dust by Cushing's crucifix, Lee was understandably absent from *Brides of Dracula* (1960). Equally understandably, he was back in red-lined cloak with eyeballs to match in *Dracula, Prince of Darkness* (1965). Once again the powers of darkness had been vanquished by the good god gold. Five revivals have happened since, including one in whiskers shot in Spain, but excluding the catch-penny *Countess Dracula* (1970). Extending this policy beyond Shelley and Stoker, Hammer exhumed a short story by J. Sheridan LeFanu, and so far have spun three features from 'Carmilla'. The first, *The Vampire Lovers* (1970), shifted the centre of fanging from neck to nipple, and as both vampire and victim are female, the future seems sexy if uncertain.

Hammer horrors have run the traditional gamut: *The Mummy* remade with Lee in 1959, *The Phantom of the Opera* remade with Herbert Lom in 1962, *One Million Years BC* remade with Raquel Welch in 1966, *Dr Jekyll and Mr Hyde* remade twice, lately with a sex-change twist as *Dr Jekyll and Sister Hyde* (1971). There has been *The Curse of the Werewolf* (1961), a *Plague of the Zombies* (1965), and three science-fiction pieces based on television's *Quatermass* serials. In quantity Hammer films are fast approaching Universal, but in quality they have yet to reach Monogram. Meanwhile they can admire their Queen's Award for Industry and scream all the way to the bank.

Of the Old Monsters, only Chaney remains.

'I used to enjoy horror films when there was thought and sympathy involved. Then they became comedies. Abbott and Costello ruined the horror field: they made buffoons out of the monsters. Then the cheap producers came along and made worse buffoons of them, because they killed for the sake of killing, there was blood for the sake of blood. There was no thought, no true expression of acting, no true expression of feeling. We used to make up our minds before we started that this is a little fantastic, but let's take it seriously. And they were sold seriously. But all this foolishness today, it isn't sold seriously. It's made as a joke, a laugh, for the kids to go in and have a ball.'

The elder Chaney, Karloff, Lugosi . . . Laughton and Lorre and Veidt . . . Rathbone and Rains . . . Whale and Laemmle and Browning. . . . The Scroll of Thoth runs from Atwill to Zucco. Yet they will be back, at the flicker of a projector, the touch of a TV switch, through their own medium – the only medium truly to revive the dead. The cinema.

So charge your glasses – with gin, of course – and join Dr Pretorius in his toast:

'To a new world of Gods and Monsters!'

Last Laugh: *Fall of the House of Usher* (GIB 1948; *left*); *Carry On Screaming* (Anglo-Amalgamated 1966; *opposite*).

TH

The Horror film industry showed no
of flagging in the 1970s, although the
ity remained as variable as ever. In *H
of the Ripper* (Hammer 1971), which
decidedly a cut above the average, Ang
Rees, cast as the daughter of the fa
Jack and here (*below right*) being se
by an anxious Eric Porter, carried o
family tradition to good effect. *The
session of Joel Delaney* (ITC-Haworth
right) used a familiar theme but, de
the presence of Shirley Maclaine, rem
a piece of unwholesome voodoo. The t
fer of a soul into another person's bo
dealt with rather more effectively in
Mephisto Waltz (20th Century-Fox
below), in which devil worship and
magic combine to make a nicely c
film.

Children with supernatural powers of one
kind or another hit the screen in a big way
in 1976. In *Carrie* (Red Band Films; *right*)
Cissy Spacek plays a girl goaded beyond
endurance by other schoolchildren, who releases destructive telekinetic forces upon
them. In *The Omen* (20th Century-Fox) an
American diplomat, Gregory Peck, and his
wife, played by Lee Remick, accept a child
as substitute for their own who died at
birth, rather unwisely as it happens, since
the infant christ turns out to be the Antichrist.
The film has some sensational horrors, including an unnervingly realistic decapitation. Here Lee Remick (*bottom right*) stares
aghast at the nasty lad's nanny hanging
from a window, while Gregory Peck (*bottom
left*) unsuccessfully tries to stab him before
being gunned down by the unsuspecting
police.

The Little Girl Who Lives Down The Lane
(Zev Braun Productions 1976; *opposite, below left*), a chilling piece of horror about a
young girl in a Canadian town who brings
death upon anyone who opposes her, won
critical acclaim for Jodie Foster. In *Exorcist
II: The Heretic* (Warner Brothers 1976; *opposite, above*) the forces of good and evil
battle for the soul of Linda Blair, re-creat-
ing her role in *The Exorcist* of the little girl,
apparently still possessed by the same demon. This sequel, like so many others, was
a failure, and not even the special effects
could make it interesting. *The Island of Dr.
Moreau* (AIP 1972; *opposite, below right*)
reintroduces that stock character of horror
films, the mad scientist, impersonated none
too happily by Burt Lancaster. In this remake of the infinitely superior *The Island
of Lost Souls* (1932), he attempts to turn
animals into humans. However, despite
make-up skills and fidelity to H. G. Well's
original story, the film fails to carry much
conviction.

Dracula (Universal 1979; above) finds our hero in England in the palmy days just before World War 1. He is soon up to his old tricks, but despite the presence of a distinguished cast, including Laurence Olivier, and some notable special effects, the film somehow lacks punch (or possibly bite). In *The Fog* (Avco Embassy 1979; *above right*) the ghosts of sailors drowned when their vessel was shipwrecked return to take revenge upon the descendants of those who lured their ship to its doom. The film generates a remarkable atmosphere of horror, notably in the creation of the 'living dead' mariners. *Love at First Bite* (Simon Productions 1979; *right*) features Dracula once again, now evicted from Transylvania and shipped off to New York complete with coffin to seek out a girl who has inspired him with genuine love: an amusing send-up, with most of the humour on target.

Nosferatu The Vampyre (Herzog-Gaumont 1979; *top*), a remake of the silent classic, has Klaus Kinski in the role of Dracula. Photography and make-up are good but fail to raise this expensive production much above the level of the mediocre. In *Terror Train* (Triple T Productions 1979; *left*) a homicidal maniac is lurking in a train full of students holding a masquerade party. The film provides an effectively gruesome version of a familiar theme. In *Nightwing* (Polyc International 1979; *above*), plague-carrying vampire bats are on the loose in Arizona.

221

In *Friday the 13th* (Georgetown Productions 1980; *right*) six young people are brutally murdered in a summer camp. The film is scarcely original but succeeds very effectively as a thriller, helped by skilful direction and lots of gore. In *The Shining* (Warner Bros 1980; *bottom*) Jack Nicholson hams it up as a writer who becomes homicidal under the influence of evil forces. An eye-rolling, axe-wielding Nicholson fails to convince and, as an essay in terror, the movie falls flat.

1980 continued with a varied selection of variable quality. In *Prom Night* (Arco Embassy; *opposite, far right*) that old favourite, the maniac on the loose, wreaks havoc at a high school dance. In the opening scene a girl falls mysteriously to her death. *Motel Hell* (United Artists; *opposite, below*) introduces us to nasty Farmer Vincent, played by Rory Calhoun, here surveying, together with his sister Ida (Nancy Parsons), a bizarre crop of human victims in their secret garden. In *Monster* (United Artists; *opposite, right*) an intelligent humanoid of terrifying appearance prepares to attack young campers on a secluded beach.

222

In *Altered States* (AIP-Warner Brothers 1981; *left*) a scientist, played by William Hurt, dabbles rather unwisely in magic mushrooms during his experiments and regresses to ape. Directed by Ken Russell, the film contains many of his pretentious stylistic quirks but fails to achieve any distinction. In *The Beast Within* (United Artists 1981; *below left*) Paul Clemens, here interrupted while enjoying a quick snack, preys on humans for continued sustenance.

The Final Conflict (Fox 1981; *bottom left*), is the third in *The Omen – Damien* trilogy. The Antichrist, Sam Neill, here projecting his evil influence on to a young boy, has now grown up and risen to become advisor to the President of the United States and Ambassador to Great Britain, and thus well placed to carry on his fight on behalf of the powers of darkness.

Poltergeist (MGM 1982) deals with a family threatened by supernatural forces. Diane Freeling (Jobeth Williams) reaches out to grasp hold of her son's hand as things start shifting around them (*bottom right*). In *Ghost Story* (Universal 1982) four elderly men are haunted by the spirit of a young woman, for whose death they were responsible. Even the presence of such notables as Fred Astaire (*below*), Melvyn Douglas, Douglas Fairbanks Jr, and some particularly nasty horrors (*opposite*) cannot really bring much life to this lengthy film with its complicated plot.

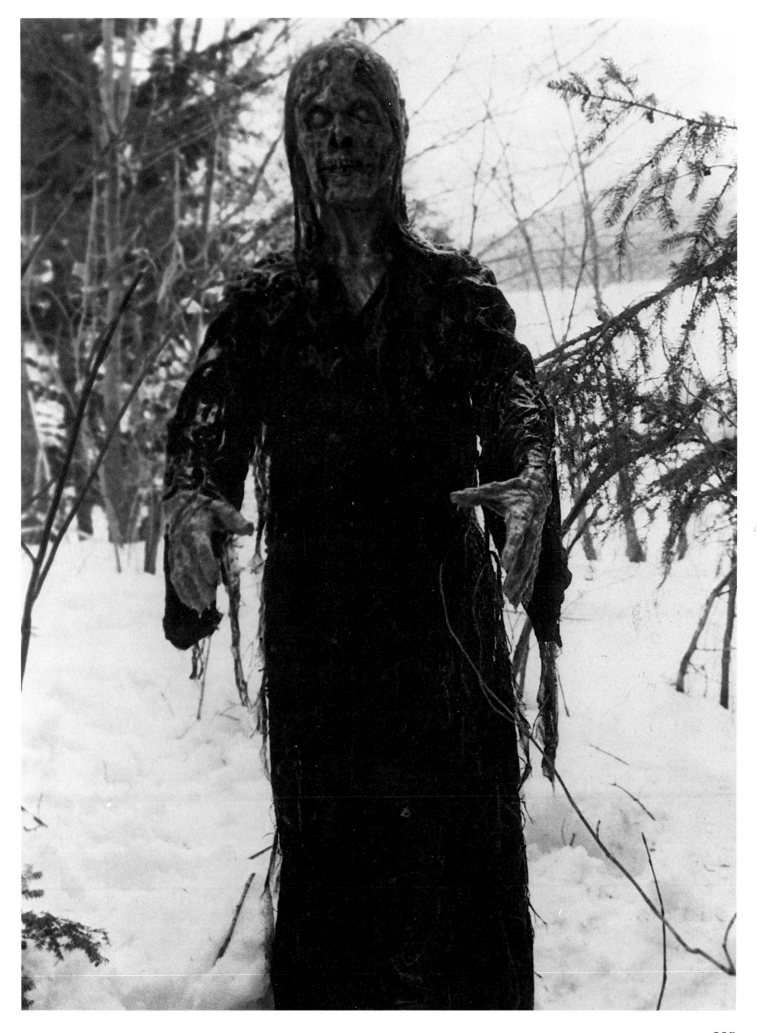

APPENDIX

The 'H' Certificate

The horror film was officially born on 1 January 1937. On that date the British Board of Film Censors introduced their 'H' for Horrific certificate, which prevented persons under the age of sixteen from seeing any film so certified. Previous to this, horror films were awarded the 'A' for Adult certificate (persons under sixteen admitted in the company of adults), but were 'notified to the Home Office as being, in the Board's opinion, horrific in character'. The 'H' certificate was replaced from 1 January 1951 by the 'X' certificate, an all-embracing category for films of an adult nature. This is the complete list of the 18 'A' films and 37 'H' films certified by the Board, together with five films banned outright.

1933
Jan	*Vampire (Vampyr)*	Carl Dreyer
Mar	*Vampire Bat*	Majestic
Jul	*The Ghoul*	Gaumont-British
Oct	*King Klunk*	Universal
Nov	*The Invisible Man*	Universal

1934
Jan	*The Tell-Tale Heart*	Clifton-Hurst
Jan	*Son of Kong*	Radio
Feb	*The Medium*	Film Tests
Apr	*The Ninth Guest*	Columbia
Aug	*The House of Doom (The Black Cat)*	Universal

1935
Jan	*The Night on the Lonely Mountain*	Alexeyev
May	*Mark of the Vampire*	MGM
May	*Werewolf of London*	Universal
May	*The Bride of Frankenstein*	Universal
Jun	*The Raven*	Universal
Jul	*The Hands of Orlac (Mad Love)*	MGM

1936
Aug	*The Devil Doll*	MGM
Aug	*The Man Who Changed His Mind*	Gaumont-British

1937
('H' Certificate introduced)
May	*The Thirteenth Chair*	MGM

1938
Apr	*J'Accuse*	Abel Gance

1939
Jan	*Son of Frankenstein*	Universal
Mar	*The Monster Walks*	Mayfair
Apr	*Boy Slaves*	RKO-Radio
Jun	*The Gorilla*	Twentieth Century-Fox
Jun	*The Dark Eyes of London*	Argyle
Jul	*Hell's Kitchen*	Warner Bros
Aug	*On Borrowed Time*	MGM
Sept	*A Child Is Born*	Warner Bros
Sept	*The Man They Could Not Hang*	Columbia
Nov	*The Return of Dr X*	Warner Bros
Nov	*The Cat and the Canary*	Paramount

1941
Sept	*The Monster and the Girl*	Paramount

1942
May	*The Ghost of Frankenstein*	Universal

1945
Nov	*United Nations War Crimes Film*	United Nations
Dec	*The Invisible Man's Revenge*	Universal

Dec	*The Return of the Vampire*	Columbia

1946
Jan	*The Mad Ghoul*	Universal
Feb	*The Lady and the Monster*	Republic
Mar	*Frankenstein Meets the Wolf Man*	Universal
Apr	*The Ape Man*	Monogram
Jun	*Voodoo Man*	Monogram
Jun	*The Corpse Vanishes*	Monogram
Jul	*The Mummy's Curse*	Universal
Jul	*House of Frankenstein*	Universal
Aug	*The Mysterious Doctor*	Warner Bros
Sept	*The Vampire's Ghost*	Republic
Dec	*Jungle Captive*	Universal

1947
Jan	*The Mummy's Ghost*	Universal
Jan	*The Mummy's Tomb*	Universal

1948
Jan	*House of Dracula*	Universal
May	*The Fall of the House of Usher*	G.I.B.
Jun	*Dead Men Walk*	P.R.C.
Jun	*The Monster Maker*	P.R.C.
Jun	*Tall, Dark and Gruesome*	Columbia

1950
Jul	*Captive Wild Woman*	Universal

Banned by the Censor
1914	*Dr Zanikoff's Experiences in Grafting*	
1932	*Freaks*	MGM
1932	*The Island of Dr Moreau*	Paramount
1934	*Life Returns*	Universal
1946	*Bedlam*	RKO

Filmography: A Collector's Guide

In recent years the introduction of the 8mm gauge (in both standard and super-8 format) has made it possible for every enthusiast to rent, and even purchase, prints of his favourite films. As a handy reference guide for the growing band of film collectors, here is an alphabetical title list of the 165 horror films released on 8mm to date, together with a note as to sound [*] or silent availability, length in reels and name of main distributor. (See 'Moviemaker Magazine' [UK] and 'Classic Film Collector' [US] for distributors' addresses. Editor)

Abbott and Costello Meet Dr Jekyll & Mr Hyde	(1) [*]	Castle
Abbott and Costello Meet Frankenstein	(1) [*]	Castle
Abbott and Costello Meet the Mummy	(1) [*]	Castle
The Ape	(7) [*]	Derann
The Avenging Conscience	(6)	Cine Service
Baron Munchausen's Dream (Méliès)	(1)	Blackhawk
Battle in Outer Space (colour)	(1) [*]	Columbia
Battle of the Giants (One Million BC)	(1) [*]	Castle
The Beast from Haunted Cave	(7) [*]	Heritage
The Beast with Five Fingers	(1)	UA
The Bells	(7)	Entertainment
The Birth of Frankenstein (Curse of Frankenstein)	(1)	Americom
The Black Zoo (colour/cinemascope)	(9) [*]	Derann

The Blob	(1)	Republic
Blood of Dracula's Castle (colour)	(9) [*]	Derann
Blood on his Lips (Hideous Sun Demon)	(9) [*]	Mountain
Bloodlust	(8) [*]	Derann
Bride of Frankenstein	(1) [*]	Castle
The Cabinet of Dr Caligari	(5)	Entertainment
The Cat and the Canary	(6)	Perry
Chamber of Horrors (Door with Seven Locks)	(1)	Entertainment
City of the Dead	(8) [*]	Derann
Comédie et Magie de Méliès (compilation)	(1)	Blackhawk
Conquest of the Pole (Méliès)	(1)	Blackhawk
Cosmic Monsters (Strange World of Planet X)	(1)	Republic
The Coughing Horror	(2)	Watsofilms
The Creature from the Black Lagoon	(1) [*]	Castle
The Creature Walks Among Us	(1) [*]	Castle
Curse of Dracula (Return of Dracula)	(1)	UA
Curse of Frankenstein	(1)	Americom
Curse of Simba (colour)	(8)	Derann
Curse of the Demon	(1)	Columbia
Curse of the Mummy's Tomb	(1) [*]	Columbia
Dante in the Inferno (Dante's Inferno)	(1)	Watsofilms
The Deadly Mantis	(1) [*]	Castle
The Demon Doctor	(9) [*]	Mountain
Destination Inner Space (colour)	(9) [*]	Derann
Devil Doll	(9) [*]	Derann
Dinosaurus	(1)	Republic
Dr Cyclops	(1) [*]	Castle
Dr Jekyll and Mr Hyde (James Cruze)	(1)	Blackhawk
Dr Jekyll and Mr Hyde (John Barrymore)	(6)	Blackhawk
Dr Jekyll and Mr Hyde (Sheldon Lewis)	(5)	Essex
Dr X	(1)	UA
Doom of Dracula (House of Dracula)	(1) [*]	Castle
Dracula	(1) [*]	Castle
Dracula's Desire (Mother Riley Meets the Vampire)	(1) [*]	Walton
Earth versus Flying Saucers	(1) [*]	Columbia
East Side Kids Meet Bela Lugosi (Spooks Run Wild)	(1) [*]	Entertainment
Exploits of Elaine (Death Ray; Life Current)	(4)	Blackhawk
Evil of Frankenstein (colour)	(10) [*]	Derann
Face of Fu Manchu	(1)	Americom
The Fall of the House of Usher (1928)	(1)	Perry
The Fall of the House of Usher	(8) [*]	Derann
Fantasie de Méliès (compilation)	(1)	Blackhawk
The Fatal Passion of Doctor Mabuse	(9)	Cine Service
First Men on the Moon (cinemascope)	(1) [*]	Columbia
The Flesh Eaters	(10) [*]	Derann

Frankenstein (1) [*] Castle
Frankenstein Meets the Space Monster (1) Ken
Frankenstein Meets the Wolf Man (1) [*] Castle
Frankenstein Must Be Destroyed (1) Ken
Frankenstein's Cat (cartoon) (1) Ken
Frankenstein's Daughter (4) [*] Entertainment
Frozen Alive (7) [*] Derann
The German Giants (compilation) (2) Perry
Ghidrah the Three Headed Monster (Japan) (1) Ken
Ghost of Frankenstein (8) [*] Derann
Ghost of Slumber Mountain (1) Entertainment
The Giant Behemoth (Behemoth the Sea Monster) (1) Ken
Godzilla versus The Thing (Japan) (1) Ken
The Golem (6) Perry
The Haunted House (Our Gang) (1) Ken
Highlights of Horror (compilation) (1) Perry
Horror of Dracula (1) Americom
Horror of Fu Manchu (1) Americom
House of Dracula (1) [*] Castle
House of Frankenstein (1) [*] Castle
The Human Monster (Dark Eyes of London) (2) Entertainment
The Hunchback of Notre Dame (Chaney) (10) Blackhawk
The Hunchback of Notre Dame (Laughton) (1) Ken
I Was a Teenage Frankenstein (1) Ken
I Was a Teenage Werewolf (1) Ken
The Imaginative Georges Méliès (compilation) (1) Blackhawk
The Incredible Shrinking Man (1) [*] Castle
The Invisible Ghost (1) Entertainment
The Invisible Man (8) [*] Derann
It Came from Outer Space (1) [*] Castle
Jack the Ripper (colour) (1) [*] Heritage
Jason and the Argonauts (colour) (4) [*] Columbia
King Kong (2) Watsofilms
The Long Hair of Death (10) [*] Derann
The Lost World (5) Perry
Lust of a Vampire (1) Watsofilms
The Mad Magician (stereo) (1) [*] Columbia
The Magic of Méliès (compilation) (1) Blackhawk
Man Made Monster (1) [*] Castle
Master of Terror (The 4D Man) (1) Republic
Metropolis (8) Niles
Mighty Joe Young (1) Ken
Missile to the Moon (1) Entertainment
Monster from Piedras Blancas (7) [*] Heritage
Monster of All Monsters (Ghidrah) (1) Ken
Monster of Death (Hideous Sun Demon) (2) [*] Mountain
Monster that Challenged the World (1) UA
Mother Riley Meets the Vampire (6) [*] Walton
Movie Milestones No. 1 (The Miracle Man) (1) [*] Walton
The Mummy (1) [*] Castle
The Mummy's Ghost (1) [*] Castle
The Mummy's Tomb (1) [*] Castle
Munster Go Home (10) [*] Powell
My Son the Vampire (Mother Riley Meets the Vampire) (1) Republic
The Night Caller (9) [*] Macro
Nightmare in Wax (colour) (9) [*] Derann
Nosferatu (3) Blackhawk
One Million BC (1) Castle
The Phantom of the Opera (Chaney) (8) Blackhawk
The Phantom of the Opera (Lom) (8) [*] Powell
Plan 9 from Outer Space (7) [*] Heritage
Playgirls and the Vampire (1) Watsofilms

Psycho (10) [*] Derann
The Quatermass Experiment (8) [*] Derann
Revenge of Frankenstein (colour) (1) [*] Columbia
The Revenge of the Creature (1) [*] Castle
Rodan the Flying Monster (Japan) (1) Ken
Seddok (1) Mountain
The Seventh Voyage of Sinbad (colour) (4) [*] Columbia
She (Marguerite Snow) (2) Perry
She (Betty Blythe) (5) Blackhawk
The Shock (6) Blackhawk
Slaughter of the Vampires (9) [*] Mountain
Son of Frankenstein (1) [*] Castle
Son of Kong (1) Ken
Son of Satan (Seddok) (1) Mountain
The Spider (1) Ken
Spooks (stereo) (1) Columbia
The Supernatural of Méliès (compilation) (1) Blackhawk
The Surrealism of Méliès (compilation) (1) Blackhawk
Svengali (9) [*] Derann
Tails of Horror (stereo) (1) Columbia
Tales of Terror (Méliès compilation) (1) Blackhawk
Tarantula (1) [*] Castle
The Tell-Tale Heart (cartoon) (1) [*] Columbia
Terror of Dracula (Nosferatu) (2) Entertainment
Theatre of Death (colour) (10) [*] Derann
The Thing (1) Ken
A Trip to the Moon (Méliès) (1) Entertainment
Twenty Million Miles to Earth (1) [*] Columbia
Twenty Thousand Leagues Under the Sea (8) Blackhawk
Twenty Thousand Leagues Under the Sea (Disney) (1) Disney
Ulysses (1) Americom
The Undead (1) Ken
The Vampire and the Ballerina (1) UA
The Vampire Bat (1) Entertainment
The Vampire's Curse (2) [*] Mountain
The Vampire's Last Fling (1) Watsofilms
Varan the Unbelievable (Japan) (1) Ken
Voyage to the Bottom of the Sea (4) Americom
War of the Colossal Beast (1) Ken
War of the Planets (1) Castle
The Wasp Woman (7) [*] Heritage
Waxworks (6) Perry
We Want Our Mummy (1) [*] Columbia
The Werewolf (1) [*] Columbia
The Wolf Man (1) [*] Castle

Bibliography: Books

Ackerman, Forrest J. – *The Best from Famous Monsters of Filmland* – New York 1964 – *Son of Famous Monsters of Filmland* – New York 1964 – *Famous Monsters of Filmland Strike Back* – New York 1965 – *The Frankenscience Monster* – New York 1969 – *Science Fiction Worlds of Forrest J. Ackerman and Friends* – California 1969
Anderson, J. and Ritchie, D. – *The Japanese Film* – Tokyo/Vermont 1959
Anderson, Robert G. – *Faces, Forms, Films* – New Jersey 1971
Barbour, Alan G. – *A Thousand and One Delights* – New York 1971 – *Days of Thrills and Adventure* – New York 1972
Baxter, John – *Hollywood in the Thirties* – London/New York 1968 – *Science Fiction in the Cinema* – London/New York 1970
Bessy, M. and Lo Duca – *Georges Méliès Mage* – Paris 1945
Bogdanovich, Peter – *Fritz Lang in America* – London 1967
Bouyxou, Jean-Pierre – *Frankenstein* – Paris
Boullet, Jean – *La Belle et La Bête* – Paris 1958
Butler, Ivan – *Horror in the Cinema* – London 1970
Clarens, Carlos – *An Illustrated History of the Horror Film* – New York 1967 – *Horror Movies* – London 1968

Douglas, Drake – *Horror* – New York 1966
Eisner, Lotte H. – *L'Ecran Démoniaque* – Paris 1952 – *The Haunted Screen* – London 1969
Everson, William K. – *The Bad Guys* – New York 1964
Eyles, Allen – *Horror Album* – London 1971
Franklin, Joe – *Classics of the Silent Screen* – New York 1959
Gifford, Denis – *Movie Monsters* – London/New York 1969 – *Science Fiction Film* – London/New York 1971
Goodman, Ezra – *The Fifty Year Decline and Fall of Hollywood* – New York 1961
Gow, Gordon – *Suspense in the Cinema* – London 1968
Harryhausen, Ray – *Film Fantasy Scrapbook* – New York 1972
Higham, C. and Greenberg, J. – *Hollywood in the Forties* – London/New York 1968 – *The Celluloid Muse* – London 1969
Jensen, Paul M. – *The Cinema of Fritz Lang* – London/New York 1969
Kracauer, Siegfried – *From Caligari to Hitler* – Princeton 1947
Kyrou, Ado – *Le Surréalisme au Cinéma* – Paris 1964
Laclos, Michel – *Le Fantastique au Cinéma* – Paris 1958
Lahue, Kalton C. – *Continued Next Week* – Oklahoma 1964
Milne, Tom – *The Cinema of Carl Dreyer* – London 1971
Robinson, David – *Hollywood in the Twenties* – London/New York 1968
Robinson, W. R. – *Man and the Movies* – Louisiana 1967
Sadoul, Georges – *Georges Méliès* – Paris 1961
Steiger, Brad – *Master Movie Monsters* – Chicago 1965 – *Monsters, Maidens and Mayhem* – Chicago 1965
Underwood, Peter – *Horror Man* – London 1972
Weiss, K. and Goodgold, E. – *To be Continued* – New York 1972
Wiene, Robert – *The Cabinet of Dr Caligari* – London 1972
Willemen, Pirie, Will, Myles – *Roger Corman* – Cambridge 1970

Bibliography: Magazines

Bizarre – Paris 1960
Castle of Frankenstein – New Jersey 1962
Certificate X – Manchester 1965
Chilling Monster Tales – New York 1966
Famous Monsters of Filmland – Philadelphia 1958
Fantastic Monsters of the Films – California 1962
For Monsters Only – New York 1965
Gothique – Brentford 1965
Horror Monsters – Connecticut 1961
L'Incroyable Cinéma – Salford 1969
Insight – London 1965
Journal of Frankenstein – New Jersey 1961
Mad Monsters – Connecticut 1961
Masque – London 1970
La Méthode – Paris 1961
Midi–Minuit Fantastique – Paris 1962
Miroir du Fantastique – Paris 1968
Modern Monsters – California 1966
Monster Howls – New York 1966
Monster Mania – New York 1966
Monster Parade – New York 1958
The Monster Times – New York 1972
Monster World – Philadelphia 1964
Monsters and Things – New York 1959
Monsters to Laugh With – New York 1964
Monsters Unlimited – New York 1965
Movies International – California 1969
Photon – New York 1966
Screen Chills – London 1957
Screen Facts – New York 1963
Screen Thrills Illustrated – Philadelphia 1962
Shock Tales – New York 1959
Shriek – New York 1965
Spacemen – Philadelphia 1961
Supernatural – Bournemouth 1964
3-D Monsters – New York 1964
Trumpet – Texas 1965
Twylight – Kent 1965
World Famous Creatures – New York 1958

INDEX

Figures in **bold** type indicate illustrations

Comedy of Terrors (American International 1963)

Grip of the Strangler (MGM 1958)

House of Dark Shadows (MGM 1970)

Warning Shadows (Pan 1923)

Acknowledgments

The stills in this book come from the author's collection, with additional help from Garry Parfitt Michael Pointer and the Kobal Collection. Stills are copyright of the companies as credited in the captions.